Sugar and the Underdevelopment
of Northeastern Brazil,
1500–1970

University of Florida Monographs
Social Sciences No. 63

Sugar and the Underdevelopment of Northeastern Brazil, 1500–1970

KIT SIMS TAYLOR

A University of Florida Book

The University Presses of Florida
Gainesville / 1978

Library of Congress Cataloging in Publication Data

Taylor, Kit Sims.
  Sugar and the underdevelopment of northeastern
Brazil, 1500–1970.

  (University of Florida monographs: Social sciences;
no. 63)
  ''A University of Florida book.''
  Revision of the author's thesis (M.A.), University of
Florida.
  Bibliography: p.
  1. Sugar trade—Brazil, Northeast—History.
2. Slavery in Brazil—History. 3. Brazil, Northeast—
Economic conditions. 4. Agriculture—Economic aspects—
Brazil, Northeast—History. I. Title. II. Series:
Florida. University, Gainesville. University of Florida
monographs: Social sciences; no. 63.
HD9114.B6T35 1978   330.9'81'3   78–18423
ISBN 0–8130–0612–0

The University Presses of Florida
is the scholarly publishing agency for
the State University System of Florida.

COPYRIGHT © 1978 BY THE BOARD OF REGENTS
OF THE STATE OF FLORIDA

TYPOGRAPHY BY CREATIVE COMPOSITION CO.
ALBUQUERQUE, NEW MEXICO

PRINTED BY STORTER PRINTING COMPANY, INC.
GAINESVILLE, FLORIDA

To Manuel—
worker, organizer, teacher

Preface

The seeds of this study were planted in 1966 and 1967 when, as a Peace Corps volunteer, I worked with the Agricultural Laborers' Union in Jaboatão, Pernambuco. As a young and naïve North American whose only prior political education had been as a peripheral observer of the Berkeley Free Speech Movement, I imagined that my middle-class education would enable me to work as a catalyst to bring immediate progress to the impoverished sugar workers. But it turned out that they were the teachers and I was the student.

One example should suffice. Noting the lack of schools on the sugar plantations, I decided that a school would be a good project—and a feasible one, since certainly no one would be opposed to education. Construction materials could be obtained through voluntary contributions raised at a U.S. school, and the sugar workers were more than happy to do the construction work if a teacher could be provided. The mayor of Jaboatão and several councilmen agreed that the town would provide a teacher. Now all we needed was about an acre of land. I was sure that the owner of the major sugar mill and associated lands would part with one acre out of his thousands so that part of his work force and their families could get a basic education. After he turned down our request for a building site, two of the union leaders told me that they had known all along that we couldn't build the school, but because I was so enthusiastic about it they had to let me find out for myself. They explained that no one with even an elementary education would stay on the plantation, so it was in the "Doctor's" interest to keep his workers uneducated.

Upon leaving Brazil, I entered the graduate program in the Department of Agricultural Economics at the University of Florida, where this study of Brazil's economic history evolved in the form of a master's thesis. Although I got the usual overdose of neoclassical economics, I was fortunate to find a number of unique individuals who deserve thanks and acknowledgment. Professor W. W. McPherson guided my work through all its stages, and whenever I thought I had encountered an unprecedented problem he was usually able to show me how one of the classical economists had wrestled with the same problem. The publication of this work owes much to his encouragement. Professor Clyde E. Murphree also read all of the early drafts and introduced me to the works of John Commons and Thorstein Veblen. Professor Neill Macaulay of the History Department lent his thorough knowledge of Brazilian history to chapters 2–5. I also benefited from comments by Professors Dale Truett and William Woodruff, both of the Economics Department. Chapter 8 was improved by the helpful suggestions of Professor George L. Beckford of the Department of Economics at the University of the West Indies.

Acknowledgment is also made to the Agricultural History Society for permission to reprint my article "The Economics of Sugar and Slavery in Northeastern Brazil," which was originally published in the July 1970 issue of *Agricultural History* and appears as chapter 3 of this monograph. The editors of *Monthly Review* gave permission to reprint portions of my article "Brazil's Northeast: Sugar and Surplus Value" (© 1969 by Monthly Review, Inc.), which appeared in *Monthly Review* in March 1969. Peter Kurz provided three photographs which he took in Pernambuco in 1963. The Brookings Institution has permitted me to use the map that appears here as Figure 1 (© 1963 by the Brookings Institution); it originally appeared in Stefan H. Robock's *Brazil's Developing Northeast: A Study of Regional Planning and Foreign Aid.*

Thanks must also go to the Graduate School of the University of Florida for making possible the publication of this monograph, and to the Center for Tropical Agriculture at the University of Florida for financial assistance while the work was in progress.

Finally, I am grateful to my wife, Rosemary C. Ford, for her editorial assistance and, above all, for her patience in sacrificing numerous vacations while I was revising the thesis for publication.

Contents

1. Brazil's Underdeveloping Northeast

In a past age, we were one of the richest and most prosperous areas of the world. Here on this soil, in the sixteenth and seventeenth centuries, flourished a civilization—a sugar cane civilization—thanks to the use of a highly developed technology. Because we were technologically advanced we learned to reclaim land from the sea, to erect solid and beautiful buildings, to prepare the soil for a crop—sugar—that was sought after on the international market. All this has been lost; today we are one of the poorest and most backward areas of the world. We continue, it is true, to produce sugar, but the export product of the Northeast, in this twentieth century, is man—man of flesh and blood, like us.

Miguel Arraes, governor of Pernambuco (1962–64)

Throughout recorded history, men of vision have cried out against the undermining of their agrarian societies by the latifundia. Plutarch, at the peak of the Roman Empire, warned that those dispossessed of their land "are no longer disposed, as they were before, to serve in the war or to see to the education of their children." He warned that if the latifundia continued to grow, there would soon be "relatively few free men in all Italy" (cited by Alba, p. 183). But Plutarch's warnings, like the warnings of Seneca the Elder and others, were ignored. As the number of slaves increased, the free population diminished. Traditional food crops were abandoned and replaced by cattle and export crops, increasing the empire's dependence on its colonies for basic grains. Slave revolts increased. The hordes who finally descended from the north encountered no resistance from citizen-farmers. Too few were left.

In the Western Hemisphere, the latifundium was born of the commercialization of valuable agricultural products for the European market. Here, even the crop diversification present on the Roman estates was absent—

latifundium and monoculture became synonymous. Here, too, were men who saw the contradiction between export wealth and the impoverishment of the workers who produced that wealth. Lord Willoughby, governor of tiny Barbados in the mid-seventeenth century when it metamorphosed from an agrarian democracy to a slave-based aristocracy, tried, without effect, to stem the rapid out-migration of the island's free population that accompanied the growth of its sugar industry (Harlow, pp. 128–73).

Cuba was also destroyed by sugar monoculture and latifundia, even though a tradition of middle-class farmers working on their own landholdings survived well into the nineteenth century. The Cuban economic commission of 1866 foresaw the dangers of a sugar latifundium that was importing labor for its vast estates: "It is a natural law that a people who surrender the cultivation of their land to others abdicate all lawful ownership; uprooted and without a future, their lives become no more than transient incidents in human history" (cited by Guerra y Sánchez, p. v). In spite of the commission's recommendations, Guerra y Sánchez felt it necessary to make practically the same recommendations fifty years later (pp. 121–56), and still without effect.

In northeastern Brazil the latifundia did not have to displace free citizen-farmers; there never were any. The indigenous population was thin, nomadic, and widely scattered. After a brief period of gathering dyewood, the Portuguese established sugar plantations with a labor force of African slaves. The sugar latifundia were free to dominate the economy and culture without any interference from democratic or agrarian institutions. The economic and institutional framework established to accommodate the plantation and mill owners has dominated the Northeast and retarded its development right up to the present day. Indeed, it was not until the late 1950s that these institutions were ever severely threatened.

In the late 1950s, under the "developmentalism" policies of President Juscelino Kubitschek, Brazil appeared to be emerging from poverty. The new automobile industry was the pride of urban Brazilians, who felt that their nation was finally mastering the technological complexities of the modern era. A new capital city, Brasília, was rushed to completion on a plain in the interior state of Goiás, a region so inaccessible that initial construction materials had to be flown in. Oscar Niemeyer and Lúcio Costa, the architect and city planner in charge of designing the city, achieved worldwide recognition. Foreign manufacturers opened factories in Brazil at a dizzying pace.

Early in the 1960s, however, the world press discovered the impoverished Northeast, where nearly 25 million people had been bypassed by the industrialization of southern Brazil. Many first heard of northeastern Brazil in Tad Szulc's sensational articles in the *New York Times*. His first article began, "The makings of a revolutionary situation are increasingly apparent across the vastness of the poverty-stricken and drought-plagued Brazilian Northeast," and went on to stress the growing power of the "Marxist" Peasant Leagues and the imminence of revolution. Josué de Castro, a well-known Brazilian geographer, writer, nutritionist, and politician— himself a Northeasterner—attached great political importance to the "discovery" of the Brazilian Northeast by the United States: "The Portuguese discovered the Brazilian Northeast in 1500, the United States, in 1960, and both times it was by mistake—an error of navigation in 1500 and an error of interpretation in 1960" (Castro, p. 3).

Brazil encompasses over half of the land area of South America and contains more than 100 million people—half of the South American population. The regional divisions within Brazil vary according to the purpose of the division and the agency defining the regions. Here we will follow the convention adopted by Brazil's regional development agencies (see map, Figure 1). This convention divides the nation into five regions: North, Northeast, Southeast, South, and Central-West.

The North and Central-West regions are vast and virtually uninhabited. The North contains the states of Amazonas, Pará, and Acre, and the territories of Rio Branco, Amapá, and Rondônia. This region covers 42 percent of Brazil's land area and contains only 4 percent of its population, most of whom live along the Amazon River or its major tributaries. The inhabitants of the North received 61 percent of the national average per capita income in 1960. The Central-West, composed of the states of Mato Grosso and Goiás and the Federal District (Brasília), has 22 percent of Brazil's land and 4 percent of its people. Although the Central-West has twice the population density of the North, it is still very thinly populated. Most of its people live on the plateau around Goiânia and Brasília, clustered around Cuiabá, or in the southern portion of Mato Grosso. Average per capita income in the Central-West in 1960 was only slightly above the North: 62 percent of the national average (Robock, p. 21).

The dynamic center of Brazil's industrialization has been the two southern coastal regions, the Southeast and the South. The Southeast includes the states of Minas Gerais, Espírito Santo, Rio de Janeiro, and Guanabara (the city of Rio de Janeiro, formerly the Federal District). This region covers 8 percent of Brazil's land area, yet has 25 percent of its population; in 1960, average per capita income was 116 percent of the national average. The Southeast has a large urban population, primarily in the cities of Rio de

FIGURE 1. Brazil: states and regions. (Map by Stefan H. Robock, *Brazil's Developing Northeast: A Study of Regional Planning and Foreign Aid*, p. 19. Reproduced courtesy of the Brookings Institution.)

Janeiro and Belo Horizonte. The South, composed of the states of São Paulo, Paraná, Santa Catarina, and Rio Grande do Sul, is the most densely populated region, with 35 percent of the nation's population concentrated on 10 percent of its land. The South is also the richest region; its average per capita income was 146 percent of the national average in 1960 (Robock, p. 21). Recent industrial growth has centered in the South. São Paulo (state) alone accounted for almost 55 percent of Brazil's industrial production in 1960 (Poppino, p. 360). Taken together, these regions will be referred to as the Central-South.

The Northeast, the "major underdeveloped region in the Western Hemisphere" (Robock, p. 1), encompasses the states of Maranhão, Piauí, Ceará, Rio Grande do Norte, Paraíba, Pernambuco, Alagoas, Sergipe, and Bahia. Its total land area is over 1 million square kilometers—18 percent of Brazil's land area. In 1960, the Northeast's population was 22,427,000—32 percent of the national population. The Northeast has a larger population than any of the Spanish-speaking nations of South America, and a larger land area than any except Argentina. With an average per capita income (in 1960) of only 51 percent of the national average, the Northeast is Brazil's poorest region (Robock, p. 21). By any comparison the Northeast is a poor region. Average per capita income ($140 [U. S.] per year in 1960) is 34 percent of the South's. Per capita consumption of electricity is less than one-fifth the national average, less than one-nineteenth of São Paulo's, and about one-eightieth of that in the United States. Infant mortality rates in the Northeast's major cities are from 250 to 300 per 1,000 live births and much higher in rural areas. Nearly three-fourths of the adult population is illiterate, and less than 3 percent finish *primary* school (Robock, pp. 46, 48, 54, 166; T. L. Smith, p. 117).

Of course, averages tell only part of the story. As with land, the distribution of income, health, and public services is highly skewed. The legal minimum wage for a field worker in the Pernambuco sugar industry was twenty dollars per month in 1965. But, since the labor contract was based on a piecework system, most workers had to work three days for two daily minimum-wage payments. The children of nearly all sugar workers are among the two-thirds of northeastern school-age children without schools. Infant mortality for this group is close to 500 per 1,000 live births. Very few plantation peasants can read. Practically none has electricity.

Geographers customarily divide the Northeast into three climatic subregions. These subregions cover only the "traditional" Northeast (from Ceará in the north to the northern portion of the state of Bahia), an area of more than 750,000 square kilometers with a population of 15,411,514 in 1960 (Andrade, pp. 3–40). The *mata-litoral*, also known as the *zona da mata* ("forested zone") and as the *zona da cana* or *zona canavieira* ("sugarcane zone"), is the region with which we will be most directly concerned. It is a coastal belt extending from Salvador, Bahia, to Natal, Rio Grande do Norte (see map, Figure 2). Its maximum width is about fifty miles, and it contains nearly 30 percent of the northeastern population on

FIGURE 2. Geographical subregions of the Northeast.

less than 5 percent of its land area. An area of high rainfall, it is dominated by sugar plantations. Most of the Northeast's cities are in the zona da mata.

The vast inland portion of the Northeast is known as the *sertão* (literally, "backlands"). The sertão is a semiarid region, producing cattle, cotton, sisal, and corn. In years of normal rainfall the sertão produces an abundance of foodstuffs, but it is wracked by severe drought about once every decade. It covers 90 percent of the northeastern land area and includes 55 percent of the population. An intermediate area, the *agreste*, has adequate rainfall for most crops (that is, for crops needing less rainfall than sugarcane does) and is not generally subject to drought. The agreste contains more than 15 percent of the Northeast's population on 5 percent of its land area. The urban and rural components of the population of these subregions are delineated in Table 1.

In the first two centuries of colonization, the Northeast, with its two sugar ports of Bahia and Recife, was Brazil's economic and social center. The decline of sugar in the eighteenth century and the gold rush of the same era shifted the dynamic center to the inland region of Minas Gerais. Rio de Janeiro grew rapidly as Brazil's mineral wealth poured through its harbor. In 1763, the colonial capital was shifted from Bahia to Rio de Janeiro. The Northeast first came to be regarded as a problem area in 1877, when the sertão was scourged by a three-year drought. Earlier droughts had been recorded, but the sertão was thinly populated until the cotton boom of the 1860s. The high cotton prices of that era resulted from the disruption of U.S. cotton production during and immediately after the Civil War (Furtado, 1965, p. 154). It is estimated that the 1877–80 drought killed half a million people in the state of Ceará alone—half of that state's population (Robock, p. 74).

The long drought led to the first of many national programs involving the transfer of funds from the Central-South to the Northeast. An Imperial Commission of Inquiry was formed to examine the possibilities of averting

TABLE 1
RURAL AND URBAN POPULATION OF NORTHEASTERN REGIONS, 1960

	Zona da Mata	Agreste	Sertão	Total
Population (thousands)				
Rural	2,001	2,038	6,114	10,153
Urban	2,240	603	2,416	5,259
Total	4,241	2,641	8,530	15,412
Percent of Northeast's				
Rural population	19.7	20.1	60.2	100.0
Urban population	42.6	11.5	45.9	100.0
Total population	27.5	17.1	55.3	100.0
Percent of population in region				
Rural	47.2	77.2	71.6	65.8
Urban	52.8	22.8	28.4	34.2

SOURCE: Data from Andrade, p. 40.
NOTE: These figures are for the "traditional Northeast," which is limited to Ceará, Rio Grande do Norte, Paraíba, Pernambuco, Alagoas, Sergipe, eastern Piauí, and northern Bahia.

future disasters. The commission recommended a "hydraulic" approach to the Northeast's problems. Dams were to be built on the intermittent rivers to provide water during future droughts; roads and railroads were to facilitate the out-migration of people and cattle. Each succeeding drought led to the establishment of new agencies and commissions, as well as the strengthening of existing ones. Although subsequent droughts indicated that all efforts had accomplished very little, the hydraulic approach prevailed. The Constitution of 1934 reserved a minimum of 4 percent of federal revenues for "works against the droughts" (Hirschman, pp. 18–50). Indeed, it seems that droughts became more frequent as funds for relief and public works increased. Robock quotes an unnamed northeastern congressman: "With such large amounts of poverty and unemployment in our vast region, politicians can create a drought almost at will" (p. 80).

The first break with hydraulic methods was the 1948 formation of the São Francisco Valley Commission (CVSF) and the Hydroelectric Company of the São Francisco (CHESF). Although CVSF accomplished very little, its conception—a TVA-style integrated approach to regional development—indicated governmental recognition that some of the Northeast's problems ran deeper than its periodic droughts. CHESF had a limited and closely defined role and became known for efficiency and technical competence. It promised and delivered an infrastructural factor basic to regional industrialization: adequate and low-cost electric power (Hirschman, pp. 50–58).

In 1951 the Northeast was hit by the first serious drought since the early 1930s. The major organization in charge of relief operations and dam building, the National Department of Works Against the Drought (DNOCS), was sinking in a morass of corruption and technical incompetence. The Vargas government of the 1930s had coped with a similar problem by weeding out most of DNOCS's corrupt elements. The Vargas government of the 1950s, however, took a different approach: the hydraulic programs were practically discarded and DNOCS was bypassed even in the relief measures. Vargas initiated the Bank of Northeastern Brazil (BNB), with the understanding that it would be a source of credit for new industries and agricultural enterprises. While the earlier agencies were headquartered in Rio de Janeiro, the new bank broke with tradition and established its main offices in Fortaleza, Ceará. The BNB represented the triumph of the "economic" approach to northeastern problems. From 1954 to 1958 the BNB did basic developmental groundwork: strengthening institutions, gathering basic data, and training personnel for development projects and planning (Hirschman, pp. 58–66).

The Northeast was struck by severe drought again in 1958. About 540,000 persons were given emergency employment, and thousands more emigrated to Brasília. DNOCS was still as corrupt as it had been in the early 1950s, and the 1958 drought gave it unprecedented opportunities for graft. Corruption and profiteering received nationwide publicity, and the profiteers came to be known as "industrialists of the drought" (Callado, 1960). Many citizens were outraged at DNOCS's blatant attempts to influence elections through the distribution of relief funds. Attempts by the parties in power, the Social Democratic Party (PSD) and the Brazilian Labor Party (PTB), to purchase the elections with such funds backfired, and candidates running on reform tickets won key positions in several states. The governorship victories of Cid Sampaio in Pernambuco and Juracy Magalhães in Bahia were important setbacks for the Kubitschek government (Hirschman, pp. 68–72).

After the publicity over graft in the Northeast and the political disaster in its two major states, Kubitschek launched a massive new development effort. Celso Furtado, a native of Paraíba who was then director of the National Bank for Economic Development, prepared a comprehensive report on a development policy for the Northeast. The creation of a new agency based on the report, the Superintendency for the Development of the Northeast (SUDENE), was proposed by Kubitschek and approved by the congress in 1959. The new agency was given control over most federal agencies in the Northeast, including the powerful and politically entrenched DNOCS. A total of 6.8 percent of Brazil's entire federal revenue was earmarked for SUDENE and the agencies under its control (Hirschman, pp. 72–80).

The Furtado policy was a clean break with past official thinking on the Northeast's problems. The structural nature of the region's underdevelopment was stressed, whereas previous policies had not questioned the economic and social structure and had attempted to work through marginal adjustments. Furtado's analysis of the underdeveloped structure of the Northeast included recognition of the role played by the sugar latifundia in preventing dynamic economic activity. The report noted that the Northeast is a net importer of food from other regions, particularly the Central-South. Transportation costs are high. However, the bulk of the Northeast's food is produced in the sertão and agreste, then shipped at high cost to the major urban centers of the zona da mata. The urban population must pay relatively high prices for an inadequate food supply that is also subject to serious shortages in drought years. This situation nullifies any comparative advantage that the Northeast might otherwise realize from its apparently abundant labor supply. The subsistence wage level is too high to overcome the infrastructural disadvantages and attract industry from other regions. Rational use of the coastal land, the region's best land and the closest to its urban centers, would lower food costs in the cities and give an impetus to industrial development (Hirschman, pp. 75–78).

While Furtado was entering a political struggle to amass more federal power behind SUDENE, others were speaking out on another aspect of regional poverty: the impoverishment of the sugar workers. Miguel Arraes, mayor of Recife from 1960 to 1962 and governor of Pernambuco from 1962 until his imprisonment in April 1964, felt that the worker who lived in the most fertile part of the Northeast was even poorer than the resident of the semiarid sertão: "He who, like myself, . . . comes from the sertão to the zona da mata, will be surprised by the contrast: the contrast of man impoverished in a fertile region which has water, when we, who don't see water in the sertão, believe that all of our miseries stem from want of dependable rainfall. . . . This leads me to believe that other reasons must exist for this immense contrast, to make the man of the zona da mata poorer than the man of the agreste or sertão. . . . It is a contrast which, with the intense green of its forests and cane fields, dazzles the man of the sertão" (IJNPS, 1965, pp. 227–28; my translation). Comparative studies of living standards in the subregions of the Northeast show Arraes's impressions to be accurate. Josué de Castro notes that while the sertão undergoes periodic epidemics of hunger during droughts, the zona da mata is a region of endemic hunger (Castro, 1965, pp. 93–247).

In addition to the federal funds promised by the creation of SUDENE, the Northeast was offered massive increases in U.S. aid. Northeastern politicians effectively played on U.S. officials' fear of communism. A Pernambuco politician, as quoted by Tad Szulc, predicted that "the Northeast will go communist and you will have a situation ten times worse than in Cuba—if something is not done. If the Brazilian Northeast is lost to you Americans, the Cuban Revolution will have been a picnic by comparison" (cited by Szulc). Before the discovery of a "revolutionary situation" in the Northeast, the U.S. aid program there had never amounted to more than $250,000 per year. In an agreement signed in April 1962, the United States made a commitment of $65 million per year to the Northeast and proclaimed the program to be "one of the most ambitious projects yet taken under the Alliance for Progress" (Robock, pp. 6, 105, 199).

For a short time the Northeast was making rapid progress. SUDENE was building up a competent staff as well as consolidating political support. Early in 1964, Celso Furtado declared that "we must speak of the Brazilian

Revolution. . . . we [in the Northeast] are living through a process which is in many ways revolutionary and which can still be directed,'' and Antonio Callado described Pernambuco as ''the most democratic state of the federation'' and ''the greatest laboratory of social experiences and the greatest producer of ideas in Brazil'' (Furtado, 1965, pp. 126–27; Callado, 1965, p. 20). Nationwide agrarian reform was imminent. The Rural Laborers' Statute of 1963 gave legal status to the peasant labor organizations on the zona da mata sugar plantations. Under the leadership of the archbishop of Recife / Olinda, Dom Helder Camâra, and two young padres, Paulo Crespo of Jaboatão and Antônio Melo of Cabo, the Catholic Church—for four centuries little more than a hireling of the ruling classes—was realizing its potential as an agent of change.

The 1964 coup decimated the Northeast's democratic forces. Celso Furtado left Brazil after his political rights were suspended. Miguel Arraes was imprisoned for almost a year, then freed to go into exile. Francisco Julião, the leader of the Peasant Leagues, escaped to Mexico. Elected officials of the rural labor unions were replaced with persons appointed by the military government. The new government put forth a cautious plan for modernizing the northeastern sugar industry (including moderate provisions for land reform), then shelved it. In 1969, right-wing terrorists thought to be associated with military and police authorities began murdering leftists, including a Pernambuco student leader and a padre who was an aide to Dom Helder Camâra. The rigid press laws prevented Brazilian papers from reporting the archbishop's speeches. Repression and terrorism replaced reform and experimentation as the dominant policy for coping with the Northeast's poverty.

Far too often, economists have regarded underdevelopment as a stage, rather than as a process. Marx wrote that ''the country that is more developed industrially only shows, to the less developed, the image of its future'' (p. 13). W. W. Rostow, who set out to construct ''an alternative to Karl Marx's theory of modern history,'' developed a theory that societies must pass through five ''stages-of-growth'' if they are to reach the ''age of high mass-consumption'' (Rostow, pp. 1–16). However, there have been several recent attempts to describe the *process* of underdevelopment—or, to use Andre Gunder Frank's terminology, ''the development of underdevelopment'' (cf. Frank, 1967; Myrdal; and Baran). The analysis that follows traces the process of underdevelopment in northeastern Brazil. Just as the process of development is often related to one or several dynamic sectors of the economy, the process of underdevelopment may center around a dynamic element. Historically, the dynamic factor in the underdevelopment of Brazil's Northeast has been the sugar industry. Even today, with all of the built-in inertia of an underdeveloped economic structure, this single industry continues to play an important role in the region's continuing underdevelopment.

2. The Historical Development of Sugar and Slavery in Brazil

Nature does not produce on the one side owners of money or commodities, and on the other men possessing nothing but their own labour-power. This relation has no natural basis, neither is its social basis one that is common to all historical periods. It is clearly the result of a past historical development, the product of many economical revolutions, of the extinction of a whole series of older forms of social production.

Marx

Discovery and settlement of the Americas was a direct result of European commercial expansion. Until the fourteenth century, Italy had been the center of European commerce and the key link in Europe's trade with the Orient. In the fifteenth century, however, ships sailed into the Mediterranean from Holland, England, and Portugal, and the commercial center of Europe shifted toward the Atlantic (Prado, p. 8). Henry the Navigator, a fifteenth-century Portuguese prince, improved charts, refined the use of the compass, and developed the art of sailing into the wind (Simonsen, pp. 37–38). Portugal hoped to open a new trade route to India. Spain also entered the quest. The fruits of years of patient exploration were realized in rapid succession: Christopher Columbus, searching for India, discovered the Antilles in 1492; Vasco da Gama, sailing around Africa, reached India in 1498; and Pedro Alvares Cabral discovered Brazil in 1500.

Before the discovery of Brazil, Portugal was profiting from her explorations by founding agricultural colonies and establishing trading stations. Madeira, the Azores, São Tomé, and the Cape Verde islands were developed as agricultural colonies in the fifteenth century. Henry the Navigator divided Madeira and the Azores into captaincies in 1426, and sugarcane imported from Sicily was planted. Under the captaincy, the crown granted

13

land to wealthy individuals who in turn agreed to pay specified taxes to provide for defense and settlement (Marchant, pp. 16–17). The grantee could then make smaller land grants to planters and sell licenses for the establishment of sugar mills.

High sugar prices led to rapid settlement of the islands. By 1460 Portugal was exporting sugar to England, Florence, and Germany, and by 1498 there were numerous towns and villages on the islands (Simonsen, pp. 78, 96; Deer, 1949, pp. 100–101). At that time, sugar was sold primarily as medicine through pharmacies—and even the small amounts produced in the Portuguese islands led to a sharp fall in price (Simonsen, pp. 95–96). The price of sugar in France, for example, fell from over 900 francs per 100 kilograms in the late fourteenth century to about 200 francs per 100 kilograms by the early sixteenth century (Lippmann, p. 365). Dom Manuel I, the king of Portugal, tried to stabilize sugar prices in 1498 by limiting Madeira's annual output to 120,000 arrobas, or about 1,800,000 kilograms (Simonsen, p. 96).

On the African and Indian coasts the Portuguese established trading stations—coastal enclaves operated by a few administrators, merchants, and soldiers (Prado, p. 11). The Moslems were already trading in some of these areas. The Portuguese were thus competing for a share of an established trade, rather than producing new quantities of a product by themselves as they were doing in the Atlantic islands (Marchant, pp. 16–17). The crown established the enclaves, built forts to protect them, and then sold monopoly licenses for certain products to merchants. The India-Africa trade was a major source of revenue for both the royal government and Portugal's growing bourgeoisie. Lisbon's commercial bourgeoisie had challenged the feudal barons as early as 1381, and the exploration and colonization policies of fifteenth-century Portugal reflected the political power held by the merchants at the time of Henry the Navigator (Vitale, p. 34). Cabral's voyage to India in 1500—the same voyage during which he discovered Brazil—paid twice its cost to the crown, even though much of the fleet was lost (Simonsen, p. 52).

Initially, Portugal showed little interest in Brazil. The vast empire, although prosperous, was severely straining the small nation's human and military resources. Prado claims that "the drain on the country's population resources caused by the expeditions to the East is well known, and the early decadence of the kingdom dates from this period and is in part attributable to this cause" (p. 10). With a population of only about one million, Portugal could not colonize Brazil as she had the Atlantic islands (Jaguaribe, p. 97). Portugal was suffering a labor shortage, and many farms and rural areas were abandoned. Moorish and African slaves were being used in increasing numbers; in 1550 10 percent of Lisbon's population consisted of African slaves (Prado, p. 19). At the same time, there was little possibility of using the coastal enclave system to carry on trade with scattered and nomadic Brazilian Indians.

Cabral named his discovery Vera Cruz ("True Cross"), and it was subsequently known as Santa Cruz ("Holy Cross"). But theology bowed to commerce, and the land soon took the name of its first product, brazilwood. The brazilwood tree flourished on the coast, and the red dye extracted from it was in great demand in sixteenth-century Europe. Dom Manuel I declared brazilwood a crown monopoly, then awarded the first contract for trade with the new colony to a Jewish merchant of Lisbon, Fernão de Loronha. The contract specified that Loronha would have a three-year monopoly on the dyewood trade if he were to transport three shiploads per year from Brazil to Lisbon, explore 300 leagues of coast (to be fortified at his expense), and pay one-fifth of the value of the wood to the Portuguese crown. Loronha also traded in parrots, monkeys, and Indians, all sold in Europe as curiosities (Simonsen, p. 53). Profits in the Brazil trade, while lower than in India, were sufficient to interest small merchants and New Christians; small-scale merchants could not amass enough capital for the long and costly voyages to India, and New Christians were prohibited from entering the more lucrative trade with the Orient because of their Jewish ancestry. As the brazilwood trade became firmly established, more contracts were awarded—without monopoly provisions—and by 1510 licenses had been granted to merchants from other European nations (Poppino, pp. 115–16).

At the time of discovery an estimated 1,500,000 Indians were scattered over the land area that is now Brazil. Unlike the well-organized and technologically advanced civilizations of Mexico and Peru, the Brazilian Indians lived a nomadic, stone-age existence in numerous tribal and linguistic groups (Wagley, p. 142). Fortunately for the Portuguese, the Indians fancied the beads, shirts, and other items offered in trade for brazilwood. It was actually the labor of chopping down the trees, cutting them into logs, and transporting them to the coastal warehouses, rather than the wood itself, that the Indians traded for trinkets; they had not established "ownership" of the forests in any fashion recognized by Europeans. The Portuguese had little difficulty in obtaining the small amounts of labor needed for the dyewood trade. The Indians were particularly fond of the knives and other bladed tools they used to prepare brazilwood for sale to the Europeans (Marchant, pp. 28–47).

The brazilwood commerce was never large. From 1500 to 1532 annual trade was only from three to five shiploads, and duties on brazilwood provided less than 5 percent of the crown's total revenue, an amount less than that incurred to protect the colony (Simonsen, pp. 61–63). At the same time, the French were staking their claim in the Western Hemisphere by raiding the Brazilian coast and establishing permanent settlements. Still, Portugal did not want to abandon Brazil, particularly in light of the ''gold Mirage'' spread over the entire hemisphere by Spain's New World mining operations (Furtado, 1963, pp. 3–4). It became increasingly obvious to both Spain and Portugal that the Treaty of Tordesillas—the 1494 treaty by which they had divided the entire non-Christian world between themselves (with papal sanction)—would not in itself protect land from other European powers. Only a de facto occupation, capable of resisting an invasion, could hold the vast land for Portugal. But, barring the early discovery of gold, Portugal could not afford to transfer a substantial portion of her population to the new colony.

In the 1530s, while Portuguese statesmen contemplated methods for holding Brazil, the European sugar market underwent important structural changes. Earlier, most of Portugal's sugar had been marketed as medicine through traditional Italian channels (Simonsen, p. 96), but when the Portuguese began to ship sugar and spices directly to the Atlantic European ports, bypassing the Mediterranean commercial centers, new markets were formed. By 1496 one-third of the sugar output of the Portuguese islands was marketed through Flemish channels (Furtado, 1963, p. 8). When the increasing availability of sugar depressed prices, it became common at the tables of the wealthy, who served large quantities on festive occasions. Lippmann reports that wedding guests of an Italian duke were served sugar statuettes of Hercules and the lion, dragons, unicorns, and groups of horses, many of them three feet high (pp. 39–40). The Flemish and the Dutch purchased crude sugar in Lisbon, refined it in Antwerp and Amsterdam, and distributed it all over Europe (Furtado, 1963, p. 8). By the 1530s sugar prices began to climb from the slump of the late fifteenth and early sixteenth centuries. Although the high prices of the fourteenth and early fifteenth centuries never reoccurred, sugar prices either remained relatively steady or rose slowly for most of the sixteenth and early seventeenth centuries, even as increasing quantities were sold (Lippmann, p. 365).

Searching for an effective Portuguese colonization policy, Dom João III sought the advice of Damião de Góis, a statesman concerned with the totality of European development; Martim Afonso de Sousa, who had led an expedition searching for slaves and gold into the Brazilian interior; and Diogo de Gouveia, a historian who had studied the Greek and Phoenician colonizations (Furtado, 1963, p. 5; Simonsen, p. 79). Furtado underlines the significance of their carefully conceived policies: "Portuguese policies drafted at the time led to the beginning of the agricultural utilization of Brazilian lands, an event of conspicuous importance in the history of the hemisphere. From mere plundering and mining ventures identical to those being undertaken simultaneously along the African seaboard and in the East Indies, the Western Hemisphere started to become an integrated part of the European reproductive economy, the technology and capital of which were thenceforth to be guided and invested in such a manner as to create a permanent flow of goods to the European market" (1963, p. 5).

In 1534, Dom João III and his advisors settled on a policy much like the one which had proved successful 100 years earlier in the Atlantic islands: the granting of captaincies. Brazil was divided into fifteen captaincies, each including from 30 to 100 leagues of coastline and extending inland to the limit defined by the Treaty of Tordesillas. The rights and responsibilities of the grantees and the colonists were specified by the crown. Among the rights of the grantees were: personal use of 20 percent of the land, 50 percent of the value of extracted products, and civil and commercial jurisdiction within specified limits. The awarding of licenses to establish sugar mills was also an exclusive privilege of the grantee (Simonsen, p. 83; Furtado, 1963, p. 43). Trade between Brazil and Portugal was free of duties; trade between Brazil and other nations was subject to a 10 percent duty. The colonists were exempted from some consumer taxes common in Portugal, such as the salt tax and the soap tax (Simonsen, p. 84).

The economic nature of Portugal's colonial land policy deserves a special note. The large hereditary land grants the grantees were empowered to make in their captaincies appear to have been feudal. However, the land policy had a mercantile rather than feudal origin. In 1530, four years before the formation of captaincies, Martim Afonso de Sousa was named governor and commander-in-chief of Brazil. A royal decree entrusted him with the distribution of colonial land, but it did not allow him to make hereditary grants; the decree was specific on this point. The land was for the use of those to whom it was granted *in their lifetimes*, and it could neither be sold nor passed on to heirs. Land not utilized within six years reverted to the governor for redistribution. That policy failed to attract enough colonists, and a new policy, again issued as a royal decree, made land grants hereditary and reduced the period in which the land had to be occupied to two years. When the captaincies were formed, the hereditary nature of the land grants was retained and no occupation period was specified (Diégues, pp. 13–14).

The *donatários*, the original grantees who received the captaincies, were not feudal barons, but were drawn from the top of the middle and civil-servant classes. Several had made fortunes in the India trade, either as military men or as commercial entrepreneurs. Six had been military officers and several had held high administrative posts in the royal government. Most did not have sufficient capital to develop their captaincies and financed their ventures by selling all of their properties in Portugal. Vasco Fernandes Coutinho, the original donatário of Espírito Santo, lost all he had in his attempt to settle that region and returned to Portugal begging for food. At least one donatário entered into a financial agreement with a Portuguese capitalist. Some were never able to raise enough resources to settle their captaincies. Only eight of the original fifteen captaincies were settled under this policy (Marchant, pp. 53–56).

Settlement was more difficult and costly than had been expected, and the donatários encountered numerous barriers. The terrain was unfamiliar and not all Indians were friendly. Duarte Coelho, the donatário of Pernambuco, wrote to the king: ''We must conquer by inches the land you granted us by leagues'' (Simonsen, p. 85). Ships were often lost in storms and raided by foreign buccaneers, and the donatários were unable to cooperate among themselves. The greatest problem was securing a labor force adequate for large-scale agricultural production. The colonists who left Portugal for Brazil generally did not do so for religious or political reasons; they migrated with the hope of becoming wealthy. Prado describes the type of colonist attracted to Brazil: ''Of his own accord, the European settler came to the tropics only when he had the means or aptitude to become a master, when he could count on others to work on his behalf'' (p. 17).

At first, the colonists bartered for Indian labor for the production of food as well as export products, but the barter system soon proved limited. Cheap trinkets no longer possessed their original attraction; the Indians had had enough of them (Marchant, pp. 20–21). Additionally, the few Indians living near the Portuguese settlements could not provide enough labor, forcing the Portuguese to outbid each other and improving the bargaining position of the Indians. In a letter to Dom João III written in 1546, Duarte Coelho complained about his lack of control over the brazilwood commerce. The dyewood agents were offering fancy goods—even swords and muskets—in exchange for labor, and it became difficult for the Portuguese in and around Olinda to purchase food or obtain labor for sugarcane planting and harvesting (Marchant, pp. 69–70). Thus, the colonist was facing rising subsistence costs at the same time that he was forced to offer more imported goods in trade for the very labor with which export commodities were produced.

The barter system gave way to enslavement. The Portuguese had been capturing Indians as slaves since Brazil's discovery, but only on a limited scale. With an opportunity to market more sugar and without barter labor to produce it, the Portuguese began purchasing slaves from Indian tribes and formed slave-searching expeditions to bring Indian slaves from the interior to the coastal agricultural areas. The enslavement policy increased the amount of labor available in two ways. First, it concentrated a large portion of Brazil's aborigine population in the agricultural centers; and second, it assured that a greater amount of labor could be extracted from each Indian.

Plantation agriculture in the New World would not have been profitable without slavery. Where good land is available for cultivation, the agricultural capitalist must insure that the laborer cannot take his own subsistence from the soil without producing a surplus for the capitalist. Edward Gibbon Wakefield, who in 1834 compared the economic and political development of England with that of her current and former colonies, related the story of an unfortunate entrepreneur who attempted to form an agricultural enterprise in Australia:

> [This enterprise] must be considered, when compared with the expectations of those who founded it, a decided failure. Why this failure with all the elements of success, a fine climate, plenty of good land, plenty of capital, and enough labourers? The explanation is easy. In this colony there never has been a class of labourers. Those who went out as labourers no sooner reached the colony than they were tempted by the super-abundance of good land to become landowners. One of the founders of the colony, Mr. Peel, who, it is said, took out a capital of £50,000 and three hundred persons of the labouring class, men, women, and children, has been represented as left without a servant to make his bed or fetch him water from the river. [P. 217]

The economic rationale of slavery and the various land / labor relationships that followed it in the cane fields of northeastern Brazil can be understood more easily if we employ the concept of "surplus product." Known also as "net product," "surplus of produce," and "surplus value" (when restricted to commodities traded for money), it simply means the difference between the gross production and the consumption needs (either psychologically or physiologically defined) of all persons who contributed to the production, and their dependents. The physiocrats limited the concept of surplus product to agriculture; they defined it as the value produced when labor is applied to land, minus the cost of the labor (Whittaker, pp. 89–90). The same concept was later employed by the classical economists, who broadened its definition, but it was dropped from general use by laissez-faire economists after Marx saddled it with embarrassing moral connotations (Furtado, 1967, pp. 78–79). Recent interest in economic development, however, has generated a need for a concept with which possible rates of investment could be determined, and surplus product—now purged of any moral implications—is creeping back into non-Marxist economic literature (e.g., Robinson, 1963, pp. 114–15).

We can use this concept in two ways—first, in its Marxist sense to analyze the causal relationships between the economic system and the political and social institutions of the society: "The essential difference between the various economic forms of society, between, for instance, a society based on slave labour, and one based on wage labour, lies only in the mode in which this surplus-labour is in each case extracted from the actual producer, the labourer" (Marx, p. 241). This is the question of how the surplus is *produced*, or how the laborer is made to work, during a portion of his working time, for the benefit of others. The second aspect of the concept involves the use to which the surplus is put. Taking a developmental point of view, we might judge a society by what portion of the surplus product is accumulated as capital to provide for future increases in both the surplus and the consumption level. Of course, capital accumulation is just one of three general uses of the surplus. It may also be distributed to all members of society in the form of increased consumption, or it may be consumed as luxury goods and services by a small class that owns land and capital and holds political or police power over the masses (Furtado, 1967, p. 79).

Systems of forced labor were used in both Spanish and Portuguese colonies. The Spanish enslaved Indians through a system known as the *encomienda*, in which Indians were granted to colonists. The colonists were to utilize the Indians' labor and undertake their conversion to Christianity. The Law of Burgos, issued in 1512, made it clear that the rights of the grantees (*encomenderos*) were defined by their use of the labor force, rather than by ownership of land (Weeks, pp. 155–59). The Spanish crown later recognized that the Indians were receiving harsh treatment at the hands of the encomenderos and attempted to alter the encomienda laws, but the alterations were superficial. Weeks comments that "once the agrarian pattern was set, the changing of the laws merely forced the landlords to seek new devices to maintain it'' (p. 156). The Portuguese colonists in Brazil, however, received direct grants of land and purchased their slaves from private traders. This was due more to the thin indigenous population than to any recalcitrant attitudes toward the introduction of slavery into the colony.

When land is so poor that working a maximum number of hours will only provide minimum physiological subsistence needs, extracting a surplus from the labor force under any system is not possible. And without the possibility of trading the surplus, the *form* of the surplus is severely restricted. Lewis Gray points out in his analysis of slavery in the southern United States that where trading possibilities were absent, the owner of slaves ''could enjoy the surplus product of their labor only in the form of a food surplus, which it was impossible to consume, or in an excess of personal services'' (pp. 474–75).

Wherever the technological and commercial capabilities of producing and marketing a surplus exist, however, slavery efficiently realizes production capabilities and ensures that consumption by the labor force remains close to the physiological subsistence level. Such capabilities can be actualized either through direct production of consumption goods or through trade. In the humid areas of northeastern Brazil, a slave could produce his own subsistence goods with one day of labor per week; the Brazilian slavery system, therefore, was based on the slave's direct production of his own foodstuffs. In the Lesser Antilles, however, a large portion of the slave's food was imported, usually from North America. In this case, the slave was always producing an export commodity, and part of it was traded for his subsistence. In any case, the slave received only the necessities of life; most of what he produced accrued to the slave owner. Since the slave had no purchasing power, there was little likelihood that the surplus produced would be invested in the production of goods for domestic consumption. This situation limited the use of the surplus to further investment in the export sector, investment abroad, or the importation of luxuries for the slave owners.

The favorable European sugar prices of the sixteenth century led to heavy reinvestment of the Brazilian surplus in the sugar sector. The Indians, however, responded to increasing enslavement by raiding the Portuguese settlements, and it became difficult to procure labor for the desired expansion of the sugar industry. Tomé de Sousa, Brazil's first royal governor (1549–53), assured the less hostile Indians of their freedom and gave them lands near the settlements in the hope that they would grow food for the village populations. Hostile Indians, on the other hand, were to be enslaved as a plantation labor force. Sousa was somewhat successful, at least in Bahia (the seat of the colonial government), but his successor, Duarte da Costa, was not able to control the pressure for more slaves, and the Indian wars resumed (Marchant, pp. 81–84).

Fortunately for the colonial agricultural capitalists, Portugal controlled the major slave-trading ports on Africa's Atlantic coast, ensuring sugar producers of a virtually inexhaustible supply of labor for little more than the cost of transportation (although the cost of transportation was by no means negligible). By 1570 there were sixty sugar mills operating in Brazil, primarily in Pernambuco and Bahia, with an annual sugar production of about 3,000 arrobas. The colony then had a free (European) population of about 17,000 and a slave (Indian and African) population of approximately 13,000 (Simonsen, p. 88). After 1570, African slaves were shipped to Brazil in increasing numbers (Marchant, p. 15). The sugar planters considered the Africans stronger and more reliable than the Indians, and Indian slaves, although cheaper than Africans, were soon replaced. Also, the Africans' fear of the forest Indians kept them from escaping into the interior as often as did the Indians (Marchant, p. 131). Indian slavery was outlawed in 1580, when Portugal fell under Spanish control and Spain's colonial laws were applied to Brazil, but it is doubtful that these laws were enforced.

The financing and marketing sectors were closely coordinated. Portuguese Jews in Brazil and the Dutch merchants were able to coordinate sugar production in Brazil with sugar marketing in Europe so that surpluses were avoided and prices remained high. Many Portuguese Jews had settled earlier in São Tomé, and by 1492 they owned many plantations and about 3,000 slaves. Sombart claims that two shiploads of "Jews and criminals" were sent yearly from Portugal to Brazil (Sombart, pp. 52–53). The Dutch, who had been purchasing sugar from Portuguese colonies since the late fifteenth century, later used Portuguese Jews as intermediaries in their illegal sugar trade with Brazil. Dutch ships carried an estimated one-half to two-thirds of the Brazilian sugar that entered Europe. Before the Dutch invaded Pernambuco, they imported about a million arrobas of sugar annually. By 1622, twenty-nine sugar refineries in the Netherlands were reexporting sugar to all of Europe (Boxer, pp. 20–21). The sugar refineries of Amsterdam had enough political power to ignore municipal laws prohibiting air pollution (Lippmann, p. 161). The Dutch supplemented their lucrative trade by plundering sugar-laden Portuguese ships; eighty ships were captured in 1625 and 1626 alone (Boxer, p. 33). During the Dutch occupation of Pernambuco, from 1630 to 1654, Portuguese Jews bought slaves from the Dutch and sold them on credit to the planters and mill owners. The Dutch West India Company purchased slaves in Africa at 12 to 75 florins each and sold them in Recife at prices from 200 to 800 florins. From 1636 to 1645 the Dutch sold more than 23,000 slaves in Recife (Andrade, p. 67).

Although vast sums were spent to capitalize the sugar industry—and particularly on slaves and sugar-processing equipment—there was no lack of luxury expenditure by mill and plantation owners. Accounts of the lavish life-styles of the upper classes in Bahia and Pernambuco abound. Boxer cites a report written by Friar Manuel Calado shortly before the Dutch invasion of Pernambuco. At that time, a considerable portion of Pernambuco's processed sugar was being openly pirated by the ships of the Dutch West India Company, yet

> that commonwealth, before the arrival of the Hollanders, was the most delightful, prosperous, fertile, and I do not think I exaggerate much when I say the richest, of all the overseas possessions beneath the crown and sceptre of the kingdom of Portugal. Both gold and silver were beyond count, and almost disregarded. There was so much sugar that there were not sufficient ships to load it all, though great fleets of carracks, ships and carravels entered and left the port daily. These vessels came and went, meeting each other so frequently, that the pilots made gifts and treats to the planters and cultivators so as to secure their sugar-chests, and yet the vast supply was inexhaustible. The delights of food and drink were the same as all those that were available in Portugal and the Atlantic islands. The luxury and display in the houses was excessive, for anybody whose table-service was not of solid silver was regarded as poor and wretched. . . . The women went so elegantly and richly dressed that they were not content with taffetas, camlets, velvets, and other silks, but bedecked themselves out in fine tissues and rich brocades. So many jewels adorned them that it seemed as if it had rained pearls, rubies, emeralds and diamonds on their heads and necks. There were no costly sword and dagger mountings, nor clothes of the latest fashion, with which the men did not adorn themselves. There were daily banquets, and equestrian fights and games at every *festa*. Everything was delightful, and this region resembled nothing so much as the portrait of an earthly paradise. [P. 35]

Available capital, a growing market, rising sugar prices, and access to seemingly unlimited supplies of land and labor converged to stimulate rapid growth of the colonial sugar industry. In the 1560s Brazil exported

180,000 arrobas of sugar yearly. At the peak of the sugar era, in 1650, annual exports had risen to 2,100,000 arrobas. Simonsen estimates that the sugar industry imported about 350,000 African slaves in the seventeenth century alone. Brazilian sugar was a major source of income for the Portuguese crown. The effects of the Dutch occupation were felt by the royal treasury just about the time that Portugal was engaged in an expensive war with Spain. From 1560 to 1641 the mil-réis had remained at a par with 7.09 grams of gold. In 1642 the value of the mil-réis fell to 3.75 grams. Dutch raids on sugar ships and the occupation of Pernambuco cost Portugal about £29 million, or the equivalent of twelve times the average annual value of Brazil's total sugar production in the years just before the occupation (Simonsen, pp. 118–20, 135, 382–83).

After the expulsion of the Dutch from Pernambuco in 1654, Brazil's sugar industry began its long decline, and world sugar production shifted to the West Indies. The Caribbean islands were admirably suited to sugarcane agriculture, and their proximity to Europe gave them an advantage in shipping costs. The Spanish Indies had been neglected, as a result of Spain's preoccupation with gold and silver from Mexico and Peru. The British and French had established military bases in the Caribbean, hoping Spain would weaken so that they could seize her rich colonies; with this end in mind, they promoted small holdings in the Indies to satisfy the military need for a large number of free white soldiers. It was primarily because of the policies of Britain and France and Spain's preoccupation with mining that the Caribbean produced little sugar before 1654 (Furtado, 1963, pp. 18–19).

When the Dutch lost direct control of Pernambuco, they were still heavily involved in sugar refining and processing in Europe; consequently, they began to finance sugar production in the West Indies. Their efforts were aided by falling tobacco prices (tobacco was then a major export crop) and a civil war that prevented England from attending to her American colonies (Furtado, 1963, pp. 25–26). The Dutch financed the purchase of slaves and processing equipment and provided a market for the new sugar planters. Also, many Portuguese Jews who were adept at sugar-processing technology migrated to the Indies (Sombart, 1962, pp. 54–55). Sugar soon displaced nearly all other agricultural activities. Free settlers were driven from the islands, and food had to be imported from North America. Tiny Barbados changed from an agrarian democracy to a planter slavocracy within twenty years. Between 1645 and 1667, the number of landowners decreased from 11,200 to 745 and the number of Negro slaves increased from 5,680 to 82,023 (Harlow, p. 309). Colbert, the French prime minister, attempted to stem out-migration from the French West Indies, but even his policy of aiding manufacturing industries was doomed in the face of the spread of sugarcane (Furtado, 1963, p. 27).

Caribbean sugar soon inundated the European market. The London sugar price dropped from 14.64 grams of gold per arroba in 1640 to 7.78 grams in 1660 (Simonsen, p. 382). Under the structure of colonial commerce the mother country always gave preference to the products of her own colonies in her domestic market. Portugal found herself shut out of her traditional markets. English imports of Brazilian sugar had fallen to one-tenth of their former level by 1669 (Manchester, p. 22). The value of the mil-réis continued to fall, accompanying the decline in foreign exchange earnings from Brazilian sugar, until 1700, when Brazil began to export gold (Simonsen, p. 382; Furtado, 1963, p. 17). Brazil never regained her position as the world's major source of sugar.

3. The Economics of Sugar and Slavery

> To speak of cane monoculture is no exaggeration of the degree to which this crop can dominate the economy of a region.
>
> *Swerling and Timoshenko*

Between the first use of Indian slaves in Brazilian cane fields, early in the sixteenth century, and the abolition of slavery in 1888, the economic relationship of sugar to slavery passed through three distinct stages. The first, from about 1530 to 1570, was characterized by the enslavement of Brazilian Indians. The possibilities of expansion under such conditions were limited by the thin indigenous population, further thinned by European diseases and Indian / European wars (Wagley, p. 142). Indian slavery continued beyond 1570, and slave-hunting expeditions were commonplace until the mid-seventeenth century, but the importance of Indian slaves as plantation labor diminished. In the second stage, the sugar industry had an infinite (for its purposes) supply of labor: slaves imported from Africa. Wage labor was available only for the relatively high-paying supervisory and technical positions, and not for the great bulk of mill and field work.

The third stage, the transition from slavery to free labor, began early in the nineteenth century. The British / Portuguese treaty of 1810 prohibited Brazilian slave trade with non-Portuguese Africa. While the treaty, which was forced on Portugal as the price of a military alliance, did not stop the trade, it did make slave shipping more expensive. An estimated 15 percent of the slaves died during passage before the treaty and 25 percent after (Manchester, p. 159). The rising price of slaves did not alter the major distinguishing characteristic of the second stage: a labor supply that was

26

exogenous to the sugar economy. But the existence of a large unemployed free population by the early nineteenth century and a slack demand for sugar led to a growing substitution of free labor for slave labor on the plantations and in the mills (Furtado, 1963, p. 151).

The second stage, during which African slavery predominated and the labor supply was exogenous to the Brazilian-Portuguese-European economic system, operated at full force for about 240 years, then gradually went into a transitional stage lasting nearly 80 years. Brazil still bears the stamp of her colonial heritage, and many of the social, economic, and political institutions of today are rooted in the slave-importing and sugar-exporting past. Indeed, the sugar industry continues to dominate most of the best land of the Northeast, and, even today, "strong traces of the slave regime are still present" (Prado, p. 4). Clearly, the sheer endurance of the sugar slavocracy deeply influenced Brazilian society. This leads to two questions: how was the sugar and slavery system able to expand so rapidly and absorb such a great portion of the region's resources, and how was it able to last so long in the face of a dwindling foreign market and fluctuating sugar prices without undergoing any significant structural changes? The purpose of this chapter is to construct, from historical materials, a model of the northeastern sugar economy from 1570 to 1810 and to examine the sugar industry's pattern of growth and stagnation.

The *engenho*, the basic production unit of the slave era, consisted of the sugar mill and its associated lands and equipment. The owner, the *senhor do engenho*, was also the owner of the slaves, animals, and equipment needed to process sugarcane. Often, the senhor do engenho was also a cane planter, but he commonly leased his land to *lavradores*, who planted cane with their own slaves and animals and brought it to the senhor do engenho for milling. In addition to the slaves, there were some free laborers, usually overseers and sugar-processing technicians. The processed sugar was boxed and shipped to Europe, and the earnings were used to import milling machinery, slaves, and luxury consumption goods. Most necessities, such as food, housing, and crude cloth for slaves' clothing, were produced on the engenho. As European sugar prices fluctuated, the engenho's ability to import goods was correspondingly affected. Each of these aspects of the sugar economy will be closely examined, with particular attention to those aspects of labor, land, and capital peculiar to a slave economy producing an export crop in a vast land.

Demand for slave labor within the Brazilian sugar industry was primarily a function of European demand for Brazilian sugar. The source of slaves, however, was outside the direct influence of the European economic system; the number of potential slaves in Africa was vast compared with the number that could be absorbed by agricultural enterprises in Brazil or other sugar-producing colonies in the Western Hemisphere. Thus, no occurrence within Brazil or the European sugar market could directly affect the supply price of slaves. With a labor supply that was perfectly elastic at a given price and seemingly unlimited expanses of land, foreign demand for sugar and the availability of capital were the only factors limiting Brazilian sugar production. In addition, the lack of alternative uses for labor and the low cost of slave maintenance guaranteed that slaves already purchased by the sugar industry would remain during periods of slack demand. Labor, during slack periods, would be used less intensively and the senhor do engenho might use his excess labor force for personal services, building construction, etc. Had the system been closed to labor immigration, the better-organized and -situated producing units would have bid up the price of labor (the wage of a free worker or the price of a slave) in periods of rising sugar prices and increasing output; an excess labor supply would have bid down the price of labor in periods of falling prices and contracting output; and expansion would have been limited to population growth and technological change.

This is not to imply that there was no secular change in the price of slaves, but only that this price was not significantly affected by Brazilian demand. Many observers reported a steadily increasing slave price as more colonies adopted the plantation system for more crops. In the mid-eighteenth century, a healthy male slave could be purchased for ten pounds in Africa and resold for thirty pounds in the British West Indies. In the early eighteenth century it had been possible to pay as little as two to three pounds per slave on the African coast. The British prohibitions on slave trading in the early nineteenth century raised the cost of shipping slaves to the Americas (Gray, pp. 366–67).

Simonsen estimates that a slave in Brazil produced 50 arrobas of sugar per year (p. 134). While noting that some estimates ran as high as 100 arrobas, he considers his figure conservative; other sources indicate that even the most efficient sugar producers fell slightly short of a productivity of 50 arrobas per slave per year. A 1639 document indicates that each field slave could produce 60,000 pounds of sugarcane per year (Andrade, p. 67). This was enough cane to supply an animal-driven mill for two days and produce 60 arrobas of sugar. According to the same source, an engenho that did not plant its own cane required from forty to seventy slaves. Feeding cane to the mill required three slaves and at least four more were needed to handle cane and to carry the syrup to the reducing room (Koster, pp. 164–69; Andrade, p. 67). As milling continued through the night, there had to be two shifts, or fourteen slaves in all. At least eight more were needed to reduce the syrup to sugar, pour it into clay molds, and keep up the fires; these eight also worked two shifts. Thirty slaves in all were needed to convert cane to sugar (Andrade, pp. 83–84). A mill used from twelve to sixteen oxcarts of firewood daily, and it was considered a day's work for a slave to cut and deliver one cart of wood (Prado, p. 455; Andrade, p. 83). More than forty slaves, then, were required for the operation of an engenho. The maximum length of the cutting and milling season was from September through April; at 30 arrobas per day, the maximum average annual output of one mill was about 7,200 arrobas. With 120 slaves in the field and 40 at the mill, the maximum average productivity of a slave was 45 arrobas of sugar per year. This productivity was obtainable with an animal-driven mill of maximum size and with field operations organized to provide cane throughout the cutting season.

Water-driven mills were more efficient than animal-driven mills, but there were few because of their high initial cost and the difficulty of finding adequate locations for installation. Of the 369 sugar mills in Pernambuco in 1777, only 18 were water-driven (Prado, p. 158). The water-driven mills of Bahia reportedly produced as many as 4,000 sugar loaves (about 10,000 arrobas) and had as many as 200 slaves (Antoníl, pp. 17–18). Even if a water-driven mill required no more labor than an animal-driven mill, with 160 slaves in the field and 40 at the mill it could have produced a maximum of 9,600 arrobas of sugar yearly, according to the data discussed here. The maximum capacity of any mill may have been about 10,000 arrobas. Because of the rapid deterioration of sugarcane and the high cost (slaves, oxen, and oxcarts) of transportation, any engenho would have had a limited radius from which it could have profitably received cane. The development of the *usinas*, the large steam-powered central mills that first appeared in Pernambuco in the 1880s, depended as much on railroads as on advanced sugar-processing technology.

Slaves were usually sold in Brazil at from twenty to thirty pounds sterling (Simonsen, pp. 132–36). This corresponded to the value of from 16 to 22 arrobas of sugar (unboxed and at the engenho) at the peak of sugar prices, and to the value of from 90 to 130 arrobas at the low prices of the late eighteenth century. Tobacco, rum, and sugarcane brandy were often bartered directly for slaves. In 1796, for example, two-thirds of the sugar-cane brandy exported from Rio de Janeiro was used in the slave trade (Prado, p. 460). Payments for slaves, of course, generated no income within the colony.

It has been widely held that the working life of a slave was short (Simonsen estimates seven years), and that the slave death rate was higher than the slave birth rate (Simonsen, p. 134). Pandiá Calógeras uses a negative growth rate (–4.5 percent) as the basis for his estimates of the total number of slaves imported into Brazil (Calógeras, p. 302). If this were true, it would have been necessary for the slave owner to replace a considerable portion of his slaves each year. However, these estimates are based on very fragmentary evidence. Records that indicate such a replacement rate (2.5 to 10 percent replacement yearly) are all from periods of rapidly expanding sugar output, when subsistence crops were neglected to increase the production of sugar; and it is probable that death rates and infant mortality rates increased considerably under such conditions. Dutch records from an engenho in Pernambuco state that 16 of the engenho's 160 slaves had to be replaced each year (Lippmann, p. 163). This was during a period of high sugar prices and rapidly increasing output, and at a time when Pernambuco was recovering from the disruption of the Dutch invasion. Records from the same period in an area that was not invaded state that 5 of the 80 slaves on the engenho were replaced each year (Taunay, pp. 616–17). A careful study by a prospective buyer of an engenho near Recife, made in 1816, states that the slave death rate on that particular engenho exceeded the birth rate by 2.5 percent (Goulart, p. 156); sugar output increased tenfold between 1812 and 1820 (Simonsen, p. 382).

A thorough study of Brazilian slavery by Mauricio Goulart concludes that the slave population growth rate was positive, albeit low. Data collected from various periods and regions all show a birth rate higher than the death rate. Goulart cites 1826 records from São Paulo which show that, of those slaves born in Africa, nearly one-third were women (pp. 154–64). Some historians have contended that the low percentage of women among the African-born slaves was one factor responsible for depressing the birth rate (e.g., Poppino, p. 159). Since the rapid rates of increase in sugar production which depressed the slave growth rate occurred only during approximately 40 of the 240 years that this chapter covers, it will be assumed here that the engenho which was not expanding its production could have relied on natural reproduction to maintain the size of its slave labor force.

Slave mortality risks were not spread evenly among the slave owners. Any individual slave owner might lose a considerable portion of his capital in a local epidemic. When the abolition of the slave trade made slave replacement more costly, attempts were made to insure against mortality risks. In 1856, the *Diario de Pernambuco* reported on the rapid growth of slave insurance:

After marine insurance and fire insurance it was quite natural that the idea of insurance against slave mortality would appear, because, for us, slaves are the major portion of our moveable wealth.

This idea was realized in Rio de Janeiro on August 5, 1854, by an imperial decree that authorized the formation of the Companhia Previdencia, with a capital of two thousand *contos de reis*. . . .

As a new institution that was unknown in this country, the company took one year to achieve popularity; it was because of the invasion of cholera that it took form and strengthened, even in the face of the great loss entailed, as it had to pay out much more than 400 *contos de reis* for 430 insured slaves that died during the epidemic. The punctuality of payment, without the slightest hesitation, or legal action, gave the company such a reputation that today it has more than nine thousand slaves listed in its books as insured. There is a great possibility of expanding this number, as only in this manner can the stockholders be offered a reasonable profit.

The advantages of the company are based on the great number of slaves insured, spread over a great land area: whereas the risk of the slaveowner is just the opposite, that is, a certain number of slaves together in the same place. Suppose that in this location the smallpox, the measles, or the *camaras de sangue* develops; in this case the loss is unbearable for the slaveowner with a large number of slaves, whereas the insurance company, while suffering a loss in this location, will be repaid for its loss by the other localities that were not attacked by the same disease. [Cited by Freyre, p. 245; my translation]

The maintenance of slaves involved little or no expenditure by the senhor do engenho or lavrador. During the rainy season, the slave was allowed one day per week, in addition to saints' days, to plant and cultivate crops for his own subsistence. The self-subsistence of slaves apparently originated in Brazil: in the Caribbean it was known as the "Brazilian system" (Andrade, p. 80). The cane-cutting and milling season extended from September through April, and subsistence crops, such as corn and beans, could be planted and harvested between late March and the end of September (Melo, pp. 74–78). Manioc, the major item of the slave's diet, was planted during one rainy season and harvested during or after the next, as it was needed. In some cases, slaves produced their own cloth and clothing (Prado, p. 256). As expenditures on slave maintenance were negligible, and payments for the purchase of slaves went outside the colony, there was neither internal income generation nor a market for products produced outside the engenho.

While slave labor was the backbone of the sugar industry, there may have been as many as 20 free workers on an engenho of 100 slaves. Among the free employees of the sugar mill were a priest, a sugar-master, a purger (in charge of clarifying the syrup), and a box maker. The sugar-master earned approximately the equivalent of 90 arrobas of sugar per year, and each of the others earned about 30 arrobas. In the field were a field captain, earning about 35 arrobas, and a number of foremen, each earning about 25 arrobas (Andrade, pp. 80–82). With approximately 1 field captain for every 20 field slaves, 1 foreman for every 10 slaves (field and mill), and 5 mill employees, a 160-slave engenho would have had an annual wage bill equal to 720 arrobas of sugar, or about one-tenth of its production.

Planters who could not finance mills became lavradores. They would buy or lease land from the senhor do engenho, or enter into sharecropping agreements. Dutch records from 1639 report that only 13 percent of the cane milled in Pernambuco had been planted by the engenhos themselves (Andrade, p. 66). There were no laws to protect the lavrador. He was completely dependent on the senhor do engenho, who might cheat him in both quantity and quality of sugar and who could revoke his tenure or refuse to mill his cane without indemnification (Andrade, p. 77). A lavrador who owned his own land would generally receive one-half of the sugar produced from his cane. One who sharecropped the engenho's land would receive from one-third to two-fifths of the sugar produced, depending on the quality of the land and its distance from the mill (Andrade, p. 66). This indicates that the rental value of land was only from one-tenth to one-sixth of the value of its production, after processing.

Land at the edges of the engenhos, and land that was closer to the mills and had been exhausted, was often planted in subsistence crops by share-croppers known as *agregados* or *moradores*. They paid in kind and could be removed at the will of the senhor do engenho (Andrade, p. 79). Much of the food consumed by the town and village populations was produced by the agregados (Prado, p. 182). High sugar prices were often accompanied by famine in the towns—evidence that either the land or the sharecroppers were used for sugar production during these periods. Prado notes that "this was a paradoxical situation, since misery and hunger lurked under the shade of prosperity brought about by these high prices" (p. 188). A royal decree of 1688 attempted to stabilize the food supply by requiring all planters to plant at least 500 stalks of manioc for each slave (Prado, p. 189). The planters probably found it advantageous to keep the slaves in the cane fields and purchase subsistence crops from the moradores whenever sugar prices were exceptionally high. As the moradores depended on the senhor do engenho for land, they could not choose between selling their crops in the towns at high prices and selling to the senhor do engenho at whatever price he offered.

According to calculations based on Dutch records of cane cultivation in Pernambuco, the yield of cane was 53.75 tons per hectare of land (Deer, 1949, p. 108). This is not an annual yield figure, as the first cane growth takes from fifteen to eighteen months to mature; the ratoon crops (two ratoons are cut in the Northeast) each mature in about ten months; and soil fertility maintenance demands that land be left fallow for one year after four years of production. As the mills of that period produced about 5 tons of sugar per 100 tons of cane (Deer, 1949, p. 108), an engenho could have produced 7,200 arrobas of sugar per year with about eighty hectares of cane land. Sugar plantations in seventeenth-century Barbados also generally had about eighty hectares of cane lands (Parry and Sherlock, p. 67). Of course, all land was not of equal productivity. The *várzeas* ("lowlands") were valued for their consistently high productivity, but few engenhos possessed enough várzeas to plant them exclusively. Hilly land, lower in fertility and vulnerable to rainfall differences, was also used. No attempt was made to use plows on the hilly lands, so their cultivation required more human labor than did the várzeas' (Koster, p. 163).

The Brazilian system of cane cultivation, although heavily dependent on the use of numerous slaves equipped only with hoes, did incorporate the animal-drawn plow to a greater extent than did that of the West Indies. According to Koster, the Brazilian plow was used only in lowlands that did not require drainage, and was a crude and "clumsy" contrivance drawn by six oxen (p. 162). While the cane cultivation system of the West Indies was "unnecessarily laborious" in its dependence on human labor (Parry and Sherlock, p. 146), this does not mean Brazil was ahead of the Caribbean technologically; it only reflects the different cost ratios in the two locations. In Brazil, with practically unlimited land immediately inland from the cane regions, draft animals were cheap relative to slaves. In the West Indies, however, land was limited: the smaller islands, such as Barbados, imported work animals from New England to drive their sugar mills (Furtado, 1963, p. 28).

An engenho needed land for purposes other than planting cane: subsistence crops, pasture, and wood. Fuel consumption of the sugar industry has been estimated at more than one million tons of wood per year (Castro, 1965, p. 102). Mass destruction of the forests led to soil erosion and serious wood shortages. In some areas, engenhos were abandoned for lack of firewood (Prado, p. 156). The destruction of the forests and the shortages of fuel that resulted were more the consequence of backwardness than of nature's scarcity. Brazil, with all of her scientific and cultural contacts coming from Portugal, was not aware of the advanced technology of the West Indies. Manoel Jacinto de Sampaio e Melo, who first burned bagasse as a fuel in Brazil in 1809, fifty years after it had become general practice in the Caribbean, thought the accomplishment so notable that he published a handbook on the process (Prado, pp. 158, 455).

Capital was definitely the scarce factor of production. Koster claims that a good engenho, with eighty slaves, was worth about £8,000 (Koster, p. 168). At the low sugar prices prevailing then (about 1812), the sugar value of such an engenho was about 25,000 arrobas. João Lúcio de Azevedo estimated that a large engenho was worth from £16,000 to £24,000 (Simonsen, p. 111), which corresponded to the value of from 10,000 to 15,000 arrobas during the period of high sugar prices when he made the estimate. This can be broken down to 1,250 arrobas for slaves; 2,500 for sugar-processing equipment; 5,000 for animals, carts, boats, tools, and utensils; and the remainder for buildings, land, and operating capital. Just the copperware used for sugar processing cost 8,000 *cruzados*, then equivalent in value to 4,000 arrobas of sugar (Antoníl, p. 19).

The prices of items produced in the colony were, for the most part, nearly constant in terms of sugar. Most service sectors of the colonial economy were satellites of the sugar industry and had no substantial market other than the sugar planters and processors. For example, a livestock sector arose in the northeastern interior to meet the engenhos' need for animals. There were few permanent pastures in the zona da mata; in fact, raising livestock within ten miles of the coast was prohibited by law (Prado, p. 216). Koster records the price of either a horse or an ox as three pounds sterling, then equivalent to nine arrobas of sugar, and claims that an engenho needed one ox and one horse for each slave (p. 168). The working life of an animal was about three years (Furtado, 1963, p. 47). As stock breeding was a satellite of the sugar industry, expanding and stagnating along with the rise and fall of sugar prices, nine arrobas is a reasonable estimate for all periods—except, perhaps, during the expanding sugar output from 1600 to 1650, when livestock reproduction may not have been sufficient to meet demand without increasing prices; and, for a short time, during the gold rush.

Some items imported in periods of high sugar prices may have been locally produced when sugar prices fell. Iron foundries existed in Minas Gerais, although on a precarious basis because of their illegality (Prado, pp. 260–63). Colonial law was designed to protect the Portuguese iron industry, which sold its products at high prices in Brazil. Since the fall in sugar prices from their highest to their lowest levels raised the prices of imported goods, in terms of sugar, by a multiple of about 5.5, there was abundant incentive to violate the law and domestically produce tools and implements which were expensive to import even when sugar prices were high. Items such as oxcarts, waterwheels, roofing tiles, and pottery were sometimes produced directly at the engenho. Tile yards and lime works were found all over the colony (Prado, p. 258).

The marketing and financing of sugar were closely connected. The sugar surpluses which had occurred earlier on the Portuguese island of Madeira were not repeated. In fact, the low sugar prices of 1500 were never repeated during Brazil's slave era (Furtado, 1963, p. 49), indicating that capital for expansion was only available when sugar could be sold without greatly disturbing prices. The Dutch were realizing a profit on sugar refining equal to one-third of the crude sugar value (Furtado, 1963, p. 9), and their role in shipping and slave trading—as well as their outright seizure of Pernambuco—suggests ample coordination of marketing and financing.

Table 2 correlates the estimates of investment and operating costs discussed above. These estimates are based on a maximum efficiency unit with forty slaves in the processing subunit and forty slaves in each of three planting subunits. All costs and investment expenditures have been calculated in arrobas of sugar. Income accruing to senhores de engenho and lavradores has not been included with domestic expenditure, as most of this was spent on imported luxury consumption goods or reverted to financiers.

The astounding profitability of the sugar industry, as indicated in Table 2, accounts for its rapid growth in periods of high prices. Nearly 70 percent of the income generated by the sugar sector accrued, initially, to the senhores de engenho and lavradores. While this may have reverted to the original financiers of the sugar plantations or to foreign merchants who supplied the wealthy senhores with luxury goods, much of it would have been available for financing new engenhos. As explained previously, foreign control of the sugar industry's profits could have helped coordinate the producing sector with marketing, and would explain the absence of the surpluses we would expect in such a profitable industry. Also, as the rapid spoilage of sugarcane prevented the expansion of any one engenho beyond a certain size, foreign control of sugar profits insured the availability of capital for the financing of new engenhos rather than for the increased luxury consumption that would have resulted from the retention of profits by the owners of existing engenhos.

The 32.2 percent profit rate indicates that the sugar industry could have self-financed a doubling of capacity every three years, had all the profits

TABLE 2

INVESTMENT, EXPENDITURE, AND PROFITS FOR MAXIMUM EFFICIENCY
SUGAR-PRODUCING UNIT

	Cost in Arrobas of Sugar			
	1610–40[a]		ca. 1780[b]	
Subunit and Item	Total	Domestic	Total	Domestic
Planting subunit(s)				
Investment				
A. Slaves (40)[c]	800		4,400	
B. Animals (60)[d]	540	540	540	540
C. Imported implements[e]	500		1,500	
D. Domestic implements	500	500	1,000	1,000
E. Total (each subunit)	2,340	1,040	7,440	1,540
F. Total (3 subunits)	7,020	3,120	22,320	4,620
Annual expenditure				
G. Animal replacement	180	180	180	180
H. Wages	170	170	170	170
I. Imported goods	50		150	
J. Domestic goods	50	50	100	100
K. Milling fee	1,200		1,200	
L. Land rental	400		400	
M. Total (each subunit)	2,050	400	2,200	450
N. Total (3 subunits)	6,150	1,200	6,600	1,350
O. Production[f]	2,400		2,400	
P. Profit (O – M)	350		200	
Q. Profit (3 subunits)	1,050		600	
R. Operating capital				
(G + H + I + J)	450	400	600	500

Continued

a. One pound sterling (£) equals 0.77 arrobas of sugar.

b. £1 equals 4.4 arrobas of sugar.

c. At £ 25 per slave.

d. The estimate of sixty animals for forty slaves is a compromise between Koster's statement that one horse *and* one ox were needed for each slave (Koster, p. 94) and Furtado's estimate that "the total number of oxen on plantations and mills may have been equivalent to the number of slaves" (Furtado, 1963, p. 47). It is assumed here that the price of animals was constant in terms of sugar and that one-third of the livestock would have to be replaced each year.

e. Imported and domestic implements have been treated as a residual, and have been estimated so as to give total investment figures which approach both Azevedo's and Koster's estimates of the value of an engenho. As the total investment was about £ 20,000 between 1610 and 1640 (Azevedo estimated between £ 16,000 and £ 24,000), and about £ 10,000 at the low point of sugar prices (Koster's estimate was £ 8,000 for a smaller engenho), these are reasonable estimates given the lack of cost data on particular items. It has been assumed that some items which were imported during periods of high sugar prices were produced domestically during periods of low prices, except for copperware. Annual expenditure on both domestic and imported goods is estimated as 10 percent of the investment in each category.

f. The total production of all units, 7,200 arrobas per year, is allocated to *both* the planting and the processing subunits in order to avoid any implication that there was a fixed price for sugarcane. In this case, the planter is planting cane on land owned by the engenho and trades his cane to the engenho for one-third of the sugar produced from it. Simonsen (p. 102) cites a

TABLE 2—*Continued*

Subunit and Item	1610–40[a] Total	1610–40[a] Domestic	ca. 1780[b] Total	ca. 1780[b] Domestic
Planting subunit(s)—*continued*				
Subunit Totals				
S. Total investment (E + R)	2,790	1,440	8,040	2,040
T. Total investment (3 subunits)	8,370	4,320	24,120	6,120
U. Rate of profit	12.5%		2.5%	
Processing subunits				
Investment				
A. Slaves (40)	800		4,400	
B. Animals (60)	540	540	540	540
C. Imported implements	1,500		4,500	
D. Domestic implements	1,500	1,500	3,000	3,000
E. Copperware	1,540		8,800	
F. Total	5,880	2,040	21,240	3,540
Annual expenditure				
G. Animal replacement	180	180	180	180
H. Wages	310	310	310	310
I. Imported goods	150		450	
J. Domestic goods	150	150	300	300
K. Copperware	150		880	
L. Total	940	640	2,140	790
M. Payments to planters	2,400		2,400	
N. Profit [7,200 – (L + M)]	3,860		2,660	
Subunit totals				
O. Total investment (L + F)	6,820	2,680	23,380	4,330
P. Rate of profit	56.6%		11.4%	
Totals for all units				
Total investment	15,190	7,000	47,500	10,450
Total profit	4,910		3,260	
Rate of profit	32.2%		7.0%	

similar case in which 300 arrobas are paid as a milling fee and 100 arrobas are paid as land rent from each 600 arrobas of sugar produced from the planter's cane. In the hypothetical case in this table, each of the three planting subunits produces enough cane to yield 2,400 arrobas of sugar and makes a payment of 1,600 arrobas to the engenho. The total production is also allocated to the engenho, which makes a payment of 800 arrobas to each of the three planters.

NOTE: All prices have been converted into sugar equivalents. This has required arbitrary estimates in some cases, but the profusion of units whose values change over time has been avoided. Although the value of sugar certainly changed through time, it is reasonable to assume that the mill and plantation owners saw the prices of purchased goods in terms of how much sugar they were trading for them, particularly for those goods used to produce sugar.

The first problem is to determine the difference between the price of sugar in Lisbon and its value at the engenho in Brazil. Simonsen gives Lisbon sugar prices in mil-réis (Simonsen, pp. 382–83). Antoníl lists the costs of boxing, shipping, customs duties, etc., which established the Brazil / Lisbon price differential. His figures are from Bahia in 1711, and they indicate that the value of sugar unboxed and at the engenho was approximately two-thirds of the Lisbon price (Simonsen, pp. 110–11). Sugar prices in 1711 were close to a median value, and a constant proportion through all periods has been assumed here, although this may understate the true difference between high and low periods. Shipping, boxing, and handling costs reverted to the financiers. While this may seem extremely high, Furtado estimates that the sugar industry was capable of self-financing a doubling of capacity every *two* years (Furtado, 1963, p. 49). During their occupation of Pernambuco, the Dutch made loans to sugar producers on the security of the crop, slaves, equipment, and lands at interest rates of from 36 to 48 percent (Boxer, p. 173). The profit rate of the milling unit (ranging from 11.4 to 56.6 percent) was significantly higher than the profit rate of the planting unit (from 2.5 to 12.5 percent), suggesting that the senhor do engenho may often have financed the lavradores from whom he purchased sugarcane. At any rate, this indicates that the capital market was subject to severe restrictions.

The extreme concentration of income, combined with the high propensity to import during the investment phase, explains the lack of development outside of the sugar sector. Satellite economies could have been generated only if they had produced something too perishable or bulky to import. Even payments made by the sugar sector to domestic factors of production were highly concentrated. Craft and construction work was often done by *escravos de serviço*, specially trained slaves hired out by their owners (Prado, p. 258). There was little opportunity, then, for the senhor do engenho or the financier to invest his profits outside of the sugar sector; the profits had to be spent on imported luxury goods or reinvested in the sugar industry. The same was true of anyone with recourse to capital, and this situation effectively prevented any significant capitalization of other sectors of the colonial economy.

The cattle sector in the northeastern interior was the only satellite economy of any size. It required practically no capital, and its rate of growth was limited by the rate of natural reproduction. It could easily revert to a subsistence economy whenever sugar prices were low enough to curtail its major market (Furtado, 1963, p. 66). The mining areas, principally Minas Gerais and Goiás, also provided a substantial market for live-

---

probably remained nearly constant in pounds sterling, and these costs account for about 75 percent of the Brazil / Lisbon price difference. Duties and official fees, which probably varied with the value of sugar, accounted for the other 25 percent.

Sugar prices were at their peak from about 1580 to 1641. The Lisbon price was above 2 mil-réis: this corresponds to a Brazilian price of about 1.3 mil-réis, and the mil-réis was then close to par with the pound sterling. Taking 25 pounds sterling as the average price of a slave, the sugar price was about 25 arrobas. While the price of sugar in mil-réis increased from 1640 to 1710, successive devaluations of the mil-réis raised the price of a slave to about 55 arrobas by 1710. When gold exports halted the decline of the mil-réis in the eighteenth century, the Lisbon sugar price dropped, reaching a low of 1.2 mil-réis in 1775. This fall in price raised the sugar-equivalent of 25 pounds sterling to 110 arrobas of sugar. Therefore, the price of imported goods at the low point of sugar prices was about 5.5 times its price at the high point.

stock in the eighteenth century. The increase in demand stemming from mining operations generated a new livestock industry in the Central-South, halting the increases in livestock prices that occurred in the Northeast early in the 1700s (Simonsen, pp. 157—64).

But it was possible for the sugar industry to survive even in periods of low sugar prices. The industry merely used its resources at lower levels of productivity. Since the price of imported goods relative to sugar rose by a multiple of 5.5 from the high-price period to the low-price period, it was profitable to use imported goods longer and replace them wherever possible with articles manufactured on the engenho. Breakdowns and delays were not as costly, in terms of income lost, as they were at the peak of sugar prices. Since free laborers were tied to the sugar system, they could be retained at lower wages except when another economic activity offered higher wages. There was an outflow of labor from the sugar sector during the gold rush; but, as sugar exports rose even during the height of the gold era (1712–60), this outflow never significantly threatened the sugar producers. In no year did the value of gold exports exceed the value of sugar exports (Simonsen, p. 382).

Furtado points out that an important aspect of the sugar economy was its ability to grow and stagnate without making any significant structural changes: "the slave enterprise had a tendency to grow in size only . . . any breakdown or regression in this growth did not tend to generate tensions to the point of changing the structure" (1963, pp. 56–58). By holding its resources, the industry could quickly regain its growth whenever prices recovered. There were also some lags in the sugar industry's response to falling prices; output often continued to increase after prices began to fall. The capitalization during temporary high prices kept output from falling for some time after prices fell. Rising prices from 1812 to 1817 were accompanied by a tenfold increase in output (1812 production was exceptionally low, but 1817 production almost doubled the previous record output of 1760). By 1831, prices had fallen to less than one-half of their 1817 level, but output continued to rise, increasing by 10 percent from 1820 to 1831 (Simonsen, p. 382).

Figure 3 is a schematic representation of the response of the sugar industry to rising and falling sugar prices in the era of slavery. The magnitude of the response (measured by the change in the quantity of sugar produced) depends on the direction of price changes. If demand conditions are initially such that price and quantity are at point A, and the demand for sugar increases, the industry will expand along the line AB. However, if demand decreases, production will contract along the more steeply sloped line, AC.

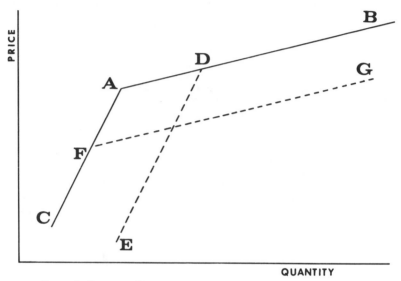

FIGURE 3.   Response of Brazilian sugar output to price changes, 1570–1810.

Thus, while a relatively small *increase* in the price of sugar will result in a *large* increase in production, a small *decrease* in price will lead to a relatively *small* reduction in output. There is also a time dimension in the industry's response to price. When the sugar producers adjust to new conditions, a new supply function is formed, and further changes in demand will move the subsequent output along the new function. For example, if increasing demand from initial point A brings output and price to equilibrium at point D and demand later contracts, the industry will decrease production along line DE rather than return toward point A on line AB. Conversely, if (again starting from point A) decreasing demand causes price and output to fall to point F on line AC, later increases in demand will expand the industry along line FG. In this manner, fluctuations in price through time lead the industry to produce increasing quantities of sugar at correspondingly lower prices.

The continuing cycle of expansion-stagnation-expansion-stagnation, with no release of land or labor during the stagnation phases, causes sugar to dominate an entire regional economy. In Brazil's Northeast, sugar took several cycles and several hundred years to completely dominate the suitable land; but, since labor was transported to Brazil only as needed by the sugar industry, sugar dominated the economy long before it dominated the land. Slavery was the basis of this form of exploitation. Where land was abundant, free settlers could not have been induced to supply cane to the mills at prices competitive with slave labor—prices below the value of the subsistence that they themselves could have earned from the soil. The high profitability of the sugar industry was a result of the senhor do engenho's expropriation of that part of the slave's productivity above the minimum necessities of subsistence. Since one day of labor per week provided the slave with consumption goods, the productivity accruing to the senhor do engenho amounted to six days of labor per week. This resulted in a concentration of the fruits of labor that thoroughly discouraged development of other economic activities and kept the region dependent on sugar exports.

4. Sugar, Slavery, and the Formation of Brazilian Institutions

Brazilian society at the close of the Empire naturally reflected the general economic conditions of the country, which in turn were determined by the system of extensive cultivation of large rural landholdings made possible by slave labor. Its structure, therefore, was simple. There were essentially only two classes: at the top, the elite, composed of the plantation owners, the intelligentsia, and the titled nobility, all living directly or indirectly on the bounty of the immense land; at the bottom, the humble masses of slaves and tenant farmers held in bondage by the powerful agricultural clans.

José Maria Bello

The sugar industry's ability to retrench and still remain profitable in periods of low prices or blocked markets was a major factor in its survival, but it was not the only factor. The sugar industry depressed living standards for the slaves—a majority of the population—and circumscribed any economic opportunity for most of the free population. The long survival of the industry in the face of these conditions suggests that its political power was considerable; and, moreover, that it had erected a political and social structure which allowed a tiny minority to obtain nearly all the benefits of the export economy. In 1798, Brazil's first census indicated that of the total non-Indian population of 2,998,000, more than 50 percent were slaves (Poppino, p. 170). Additionally, a large and rapidly expanding portion of the free-white and mulatto population was a "socially undefined element" composed of "unclassified individuals" (Prado, p. 328). As a class, the senhores de engenho showed remarkable abilities in social control that were at least as important as their abilities as agriculturalists and enterprise managers.

At this point it would be helpful to clarify some differences between two systems of economic thought. Orthodox Western economists generally ascribe "productivity" to the individual or corporate producing enterprise. Within the producing enterprise, productivity is divided among individual and identifiable resources (generally land, labor, and capital). Under conditions of perfect competition, the owner of the resources is paid for their use in a manner commensurate with the contribution they make to production. Deviations from the conditions of perfect competition cause distortions in compensation and give an unearned return to the resource owner who is able to monopolize resources. Some classical economists, however, have recognized that land monopolies call for correction through appropriate public policies. John Stuart Mill, for example, argued for an Irish land reform: "The land of Ireland, the land of every country, belongs to the people of that country. The individuals called landowners have no right, in morality and justice, to any thing but the rent, or compensation for its saleable value. With regard to the land itself, the paramount consideration is, by what mode of appropriation and of cultivation it can be made most useful to the collective body of its inhabitants" (p. 441). Still, the classical economists and their modern-day followers—with notable exceptions— have based their analytical system on perfect competition and have regarded deviations from it as special cases.

The institutional economists ascribe productivity to society in general, then note that the complexity of economic and political interrelationships which determine price prevent the value of any single factor of production from being isolated and measured. They believe that the individual shares in the total social production in accordance with his ability to exert pressure on society, not in accordance with his productivity (which is unmeasurable). *Coercion is central to economic activity.* Gambs calls this the "hidden premise" and the "genuinely identifying badge of institutionalism" (pp. 11–15). To understand how the senhores de engenho appropriated such a large portion of the total social product, we must investigate their means of coercion.

In its purest form, the master / slave relationship is a relationship of force. As property, the slave has no choice but to carry out the orders of the master. Yet the master must constantly make the slave aware of the master's superior physical power. If the threat of the whip is strong enough, or if the slave accepts the dominant position of the master as the natural order, the whip will not often be needed. The senhor do engenho's problem was to maintain dominance over slaves who greatly outnumbered him. Hiring enough overseers to keep the slaves in immediate fear would be too costly. The overseers could themselves become a threat to the senhor do engenho's dominant position if they were not paid enough to believe they were bene-fiting from slavery. The senhores de engenho could only survive *as a class* if they successfully created an institutional structure in which the free poor accepted the dominance of the senhores; the slaves would not often test the senhores' power; and the state would use its military, legal, and police powers to defend the interests of the senhores.

Development of an institutional system based on the supremacy of private property is a dual process. One side is the legal and economic structure through which economic force comes to be substituted for physical force. Property becomes both the foundation and the source of economic power. This can be analyzed in terms of John Commons's distinction between duress and coercion. By making property the means of controlling the society, the *ends* of property ownership also become the *means* of guaranteeing control over profitable resources. The other side of institutional development is the method used by the dominant class to establish its *legitimacy* in the eyes of the populace. Weber calls this ''the institutionalization of authority.'' By this two-step process, the need for overt physical force in the pursuit of private profit is diminished. Through a legal and institutional framework, property becomes the basis of power over productive resources. Then property becomes institutionalized as an authority in its own right: both the concept of private property and the legitimacy of the dominant class as the owners of property come to be above question and are accepted by those who do not own property and even by those who are property.

John Commons's differentiation between duress and coercion in economic affairs provides an analytical framework particularly well suited to the analysis of the institutional development of the Brazilian sugar economy. Commons uses a Robinson Crusoe setting:

> Suppose there are two persons on the island—Crusoe and Friday. Neither has any alternative opportunity but must deal with the other or else get along with his own isolated labor. There is no government to enforce rights or protect liberties. Each relies on his own power, and the things which each holds as his own product are anything needed by the other.
>
> Two kinds of coercion are conceivable, which we distinguish as Duress and Coercion. Both parties resort to violence. The stronger robs the weaker. Duress. Afterwards, without violence, the stronger continues to rob the weaker by threats of violence. Duress is not only violence—it is also the threat of violence. Violence is the alternative, the inducement. The duressed individual is offered two alternatives and chooses the less onerous. . . .

But suppose each of the parties is physically the equal of the other. Two Crusoes. Violence and threats of violence are nullified by equalization. Each wants or needs what the other produces and holds. Each has the equal degree of physical power to withhold from the other. Each now submits to the other a different set of alternatives. The alternatives now are not the duress of violence but the scarcity of going without what he needs but which the other withholds.

But the power of scarcity, like the power of duress, may be unequal. This is what we mean by Coercion. It depends on the relative wants and resources of the opposite parties. But, since resources are but the means of satisfying the corresponding wants, and since the satisfying of wants exhausts resources in course of time, the power of each to determine the ratios of exchange depends upon their relative power to wait for the other to give in. The one with larger resources or less wants can wait longer than the other. He has the larger power of abundance which gives him larger power of waiting and can eventually impose a higher value on his own product in terms of exchange for a larger quantity of the services of the other. . . .

Suppose population surrounds Crusoe and Friday and that a government rules them. Physical duress now is equalized, not by supposition, but by government. Friday may be the slave of Crusoe, not because Crusoe is physically, economically, or morally superior, but because the state compels Friday to obey and it both relieves Crusoe of dependence on his own doubtful superior power and excludes third parties from offering to Friday alternative opportunities. Whether Crusoe persuades, coerces, or whips Friday is a matter of indifference, for Friday is a thing, not a citizen, and the only relation between them is the managerial transaction of command and obedience, not the bargaining transactions of buying and selling.

But suppose the state grants to Friday personal and property rights—passes the Thirteenth and Fourteenth Amendments; converts him to a citizen. What it grants, from the economic standpoint, is equal physical power to withhold services and products. Physical force is presumably eliminated by equality of citizenship and a judiciary. Private violence and the private threats of violence are prohibited, and only sovereignty threatens and exercises physical duress. Each must now resort to the economic coercion of waiting until the other gives in. [1959, pp. 336–38]

Before abolition, the senhores de engenho depended on the state to protect their position vis-à-vis the slaves, thus eliminating the need for large private police forces. The senhores also depended on the institution of private property to maintain their position vis-à-vis the free poor. The agregados and moradores who lived on the fringes of the sugar plantations had, in Commons's terminology, no power to wait: they had to make sharecropping bargains on the landowner's terms. Monopoly of the land by one small class also restricted the opportunities available to the nonagricultural poor, many of whom had to serve in the army because there were so few alternatives. No unowned land was available close to markets. After abolition, property in land also became the basis of control over the former slaves.

With private property established as the basis of power, the senhor do engenho could extend and transmit this power only by maintaining the integrity of the producing unit—the engenho with its lands, slaves, buildings, and capital equipment. In Europe, primogeniture had been an important method of transmitting power since the fall of the Roman Empire. The significance of primogeniture, according to Adam Smith, was that "when land was considered as the means, not of subsistence merely, but of power and protection, it was thought better that it should descend undivided to one" (p. 361).

In Brazil, the vastness of the land gave a special flavor to primogeniture. The family was the basis of the transmission and extension of power and wealth. While the engenho was rarely broken up and was passed intact to the eldest son, other sons and daughters often received new engenhos formed on the original land grant. There was considerable intermarriage within the landowning class, and a marriage was often celebrated with the founding of a new engenho. The original land grant, the *sesmaria*, was usually from 10,000 to 13,000 hectares; however, by late in the nineteenth century, most engenhos covered only from 200 to 1,000 hectares (Andrade, p. 101). The core family extended itself through the subdivision of land and the formation of new engenhos, while the original engenho was passed intact to the eldest son and its division was forbidden by contract (Azevedo, 1950, p. 92). Of the twenty-six engenhos around Cabo (Pernambuco) mentioned by Felipe, eight were established by João Pais Barreto and his descendants (Felipe, pp. 150–55). Engenho Jurissaca was founded in 1626 by Barreto as a wedding gift to his daughter. Jurissaca was established as a *morgado*, a legal arrangement guaranteeing that it would be passed intact to the firstborn son (Felipe, p. 152).

Recognition of property as the basis of economic power does not completely explain how a few senhores de engenho were able to control so many slaves and free poor. We still need to find the basis of property. Property, as a legal relationship, requires the existence of a state with the power and the will to protect property. Property, as a social relationship, requires acceptance of the institution of private property by a large portion of the population; without such acceptance, a regime based on property is endangered by revolution. Here Weber's definitions of "power," "imperative control," and "discipline" are useful: " 'Power' . . . is the probability that one actor within a social relationship will be in a position to carry out his own will despite resistance, regardless of the basis on which this probability rests. 'Imperative control' . . . is the probability that a command with a given specific content will be obeyed by a given group of persons. 'Discipline' is the probability that by virtue of habituation a command will receive prompt and automatic obedience in stereotyped forms, on the part of a given group of persons" (p. 152). While power can rest on physical force, discipline—which Weber further defines as "uncritical and unresisting mass obedience"—depends on the commanded's acceptance of the authority of the commander. Both imperative control and discipline imply institutionalization of relationships that limit the scope of the commands. These relationships often stem from each class's acceptance of its traditional role in society.

According to Weber, every social system "attempts to establish and to cultivate the belief in its 'legitimacy' " (p. 325). *Legitimacy* means the degree to which the existing social order is accepted as the natural order. The institutionalization of authority is one means by which the dominant class extends its power and mitigates the need to meet day-to-day challenges to its authority from other socioeconomic classes. Weber distinguishes three "pure types" of legitimacy—legal, traditional, and charismatic—but maintains that "none of these three ideal types . . . is usually to be found in historical cases in 'pure' form" (p. 329). The legitimacy of the Brazilian senhor do engenho was based on a mixture of law and tradition.

It makes little difference whether we follow the terminology of Weber or of the Marxist sociologists. Horowitz, for example, claims that "Weber turned Marx upside down." He would substitute "illegitimacy" for Weber's "legitimacy" where Latin America is concerned (1969, p. 4). Whichever term we use, there is little doubt that through the institutionalization of authority the senhores de engenho were able to maintain their positions of power and privilege at less cost than if they had based their positions on police power alone. Horowitz's comments on modern Latin America apply with equal force to colonial Brazil: "It is important to distinguish between illegitimacy and violence. Latin American societies operating in terms of the norm of illegitimacy, while often prone to greater outbursts of mass violence, just as often display an institutionalization of illegitimacy which drastically reduces the amount (and certainly the quality) of violence manifest in them" (1969, p. 5).

The development of the sociopolitical institutional framework of northeastern Brazil is of more than historical interest. Much of it still exists. Even though slavery was abolished in 1888, many attitudes and institutions associated with slavery still dominate the region. Institutions do not disappear with the economic systems that created them. They remain, with diminished force perhaps, to give distinctive shape to the new economic systems that rise from the old. "Psychological dispositions and social structures acquired in the dim past," writes Schumpeter, "once firmly established, tend to maintain themselves and to continue in effect long after they have lost their meaning and their life-preserving function" (pp. 83–84). José Maria Bello comments that the sugar industry, having created "a large class of proud and powerful feudal masters, who were virtually independent of the metropolitan state, . . . set the pattern of Brazilian society, which is only now [1954] being threatened by that of urban industrial civilization" (p. 7).

With this in mind, we may ask why Brazil did not inherit a set of developed Portuguese institutions. What freedom did the upper class have to frame the colonial society and to what degree were they slaves to Iberian attitudes and sociopolitical structures? Three hypotheses help to explain the ability of the colonists to establish institutional structures so deep that they affected even the food habits of the slaves. These are: Ayres's hypothesis of the dynamic qualities of a frontier; Prado's hypothesis of the commercial nature of Brazilian slavery in comparison with the evolutionary slavery of Greece and Rome; and Schumpeter's theory about the ability of a once-successful class to entrench itself into a long-lived position of power.

A frontier, writes Ayres, is "a region into which people come from another and older center of their older life, bringing with them the tools and materials of their older life, their cereal plants and vines and fruit trees, their domestic animals and accouterments, their techniques of working stone and wood and their architectural designs and all the rest" (p. 133). They also bring, he adds, their "immemorial beliefs and 'values,' their mores and folkways." But the "conditions of frontier life" take a heavy toll on the mores. New attitudes arise to cope with new conditions, new productive processes are developed, and new social institutions are formed. The senhores de engenho, in the relative isolation of their plantations, had the opportunity to mold the plantation social structure and thereby to mold the colonial social structure. They were not to be judged by the mores of Portugal. In other circumstances the padre would be a teacher of older values, but in Brazil he was another plantation employee. Concerned more with ritual and his own business affairs than with beliefs, the colonial padre seems "never to have seriously considered providing proper religious instruction" (Prado, p. 413).

Prado contrasted the commercial nature of Brazilian slavery with the evolutionary nature of Greek and Roman slavery. The slave of the ancient world had a socially defined role established through centuries of social and economic evolution; he was part of the coordinated development of total society. New World slavery, on the other hand, "came into existence abruptly, without any link with the past or a long tradition" (Prado, pp. 313–17). The absence of tradition gave the dominant class the opportunity to establish new traditions based only on sugar cultivation and processing. The preponderance of males among the Portuguese settlers led to a sexual, as well as economic, role for the female slave. While the slave in the ancient world corresponded to the wage laborer in modern society, the economic role of the New World slave was in contrast to the role of free wage laborers or sharecroppers in the same society (Prado, p. 314). The slave of the ancient world was "never simply the brutal and mindless labor machine that his American successor was to become" (Prado, p. 316). The market orientation of Brazilian agriculture led to the dehumanization of the slave. Throughout history, slaves producing for an external market have been worked much harder than slaves producing for relatively self-sufficient estates with limited consumption possibilities (Mandel, p. 135).

Schumpeter's analysis of the tenacity of a once-successful group could have been written with the Brazilian sugar barons in mind:

> Success, once achieved, exerts a continuing effect, without further accomplishment, for two reasons: First of all, the prestige it engenders assumes a life of its own. It does not necessarily disappear when its basis disappears—nor, for that matter, does its basis readily disappear. *This is the very heart and soul of the independent organic existence of "class."* In the second place, in the vast majority of cases success brings in its wake important functional positions and other powers over material resources. The position of the physical individual becomes entrenched, and with it that of the family. . . . This opens up further opportunities to the family. . . . *Coordinate families then merge into a social class, welded together by a bond, the substance of which we now understand. This relationship assumes a life of its own and is then able to grant protection and confer prestige.* [Pp. 218–19; italics Schumpeter's]

The senhores de engenho were in positions of power from the moment they formed their plantations and built their mills. Indeed, most migrated to Brazil with the understanding that they would own large areas of land and control sizable labor forces. Prado notes that "the European settler came to the tropics only when he could be in a position of command, when he had the means or aptitude to become a master, when he could count on others to work on his behalf'' (Prado, p. 17). Thus, the sugar barons were able to influence Brazil's sociopolitical structure from the beginning of its history as a sugar-producing colony.

There were five different groups with which the senhor do engenho had contact: his own class, the state, the slaves, the free poor, and the merchants and other wealthy colonists. Conflicts of interest could—and did—arise with all of them. Relationships within his own class were of paramount importance; cohesion and similarity of interests among the members of this class gave him power which he could not have wielded alone. Next in importance were his relationships with the state—with Portugal and her colonial governors until 1822, then with the independent government. The state granted land, established the duties on sugar, protected him from foreign and Indian invasions, built harbors, and sent troops to destroy the inland colonies formed by runaway slaves. His relationships with the slaves were the basis of his economic strength; he wanted a docile and disciplined labor force. The free poor were the sharecroppers, who grew some of his food; the soldiers, who represented his physical power over the slaves; and the overseers, foremen, and city and port workers without whom his sugar would be worthless. Last were those members of the colonial society who were neither poor nor sugar barons. These were primarily merchants, cattle ranchers, and others who supplied the plantations with capital goods, consumption goods, and loaned money.

While the intermarriage of engenho families and the expansion of the family insured the dominant position of the senhor do engenho, the acculturation process within the family was also important to the long-term survival of the land-owning class. The family was patriarchal, and the senhor expected unquestioning obedience from his wife and children. The sons were not to question the dominance of the father and were expected to accept the social structure as natural and unchangeable, as they would expect to be obeyed when they attained the position of senhor do engenho. It was particularly important that no members of the slaveholding class question the morality of slavery. After abolition, the same attitude of rightful dominance was extended to the free labor force. In his autobiographical novel *Plantation Boy*, José Lins do Rêgo writes: ''I got so used to seeing these people every day in their degradation and misery that I accepted their state as something natural. As a young boy I never felt sorry for them. I thought it quite natural to see them living and sleeping in a pigsty, having nothing to eat, and working like beasts of burden. My understanding of life at that time made me accept all this as part of God's plan. They had been born like this because God had wanted it that way, just like God had wanted us to be born white and to rule over them. Did we not also rule over the cattle, the donkeys, the fields, and the forests?'' (p. 80).

The sugar industry's relationships with the state were simplified by the state's recognition of it as the agricultural arm of the state. The colonial political structure had two distinct poles: the Portuguese crown, giving it juridical form, and the engenho, giving it substantive form (Azevedo, 1958, p. 14). The crown made land grants, provided the engenhos with military aid, fixed sugar prices, acted as an intermediary in all dealings with non-Portuguese Europe, and organized the fleets that transported the sugar to Lisbon. The sugar barons were licensed agents of the crown, paying for this privilege with 10 percent of their produce. This relationship continued, in modified form, into the first few years of independence. In 1827 laissez-faire attitudes came into prominence; licenses were no longer required to establish a mill and sugar prices were left to the market (Azevedo, 1958, pp. 143–44).

Other aspects of the colonial administration indirectly extended and secured the power of the senhores. Agricultural taxes, 10 percent of the total produce, were collected in cash and could not be paid in kind. Subsistence farmers were forced to borrow cash for their tax payments from the wealthy senhores and urban moneylenders. This left their lands and crops in continually precarious circumstances. The tax structure was responsible for scattering a portion of the population into the hinterlands beyond the reach of the tax contractors (Prado, p. 377). The tax contractors generally demanded three years' taxes at one time. Generally, the Brazilian tax system discouraged the development of a rural middle class of free farmers.

The slaves were, as Antoníl remarked, ''the hands and the feet of the senhor do engenho'' (p. 91). The wealth and status of the senhor depended on his control over the captive labor force. While armed force and close supervision were the root of his power, control also depended significantly on the acceptance of the social system by the slaves. The African slaves were often terrified of their new environment, and this fear helped the senhor do engenho. The senhores composed their labor forces from as many tribes and linguistic groups as possible to thwart development of social organization among the slaves (da Costa, pp. 150–51).

One nineteenth-century visitor described the two principles of slave discipline as ''that of the whip and that of the dogma, that of the foreman and that of the priest.'' The priests taught the slaves to be obedient and resigned to their fates. The slaves learned that they were sons of the devil—a condemned race whose only hope of salvation lay in obedient service to the white masters:

> All slaves in Brazil follow the religion of their masters; and notwithstanding the impure state in which the Christian church exists in that country, still such are the beneficent effects of the Christian religion that these, its adopted children, are improved by it to an infinite degree; and the slave who attends to the strict observance of religious ceremonies invariably proves to be a good servant. The Africans who are imported from Angola are baptized in lots before they leave their own shores, and on their arrival to Brazil they are to learn the doctrines of the church, and the duties of the religion into which they have entered. The unbaptized Negro feels that he is considered as an inferior being, and therefore he is desirous of being made equal to his companions. . . .
>
> The excitement of devout feelings among the slaves, even of those feelings which are produced by the Roman Catholic religion, cannot fail to be serviceable; and if men are to exist as slaves, this is doubtless the religion which is best adapted to persons in a state of subjection. [Koster, pp. 128, 179]

When religion failed, physical punishment was used. Whipping was common. A stock was standard equipment on nearly every engenho. Shackles, brass and iron masks, and imprisonment were also used liberally (da Costa, pp. 150–54).

Although open slave revolts were rare, it was common for slaves to escape and form colonies, called *quilombos*, in the backlands. The existence of a nearby quilombo often enticed other slaves to escape, and known quilombos were destroyed by government troops. The Republic of Palmares, Brazil's best-known quilombo, survived for more than sixty years in the backlands of the Northeast's sugar region. Palmares was finally destroyed in 1694 after a long series of previous military campaigns had failed to root out the slaves. Palmares was an important political issue in Pernambuco and Alagoas because its members would sneak back to the engenhos to help other slaves escape (E. Carneiro, pp. 49–52). Many slave owners employed private slave-hunters to seek their runaway slaves (da Costa, p. 152).

The senhores de engenho depended on the free population in many ways. The militia was composed primarily of sharecroppers and could be called up at the whim of the powerful senhores (Boxer, p. 112); one unsuccessful campaign against Palmares involved 400 soldiers (E. Carneiro, p. 117). The engenhos were operated by the many categories of free labor described in chapter 3, and most senhores increased their power by surrounding their estates with sharecroppers (Prado, p. 329). Generally, however, a free population has a limited role in a slave society. There was no land available near the populated sugar region, so a free worker could only become an independent farmer by abandoning all market relationships and taking up subsistence farming in the backlands. Living on scattered plots of land, away from the center of the engenho and other sharecroppers, the agregados and moradores could not exert any lasting political pressure on the highly stratified class structure.

The relationships of the senhores de engenho with the merchants of the cities were not always harmonious. Their conflicts took several forms—for example, the type of social rivalry that is common between rural and urban cultures. The senhores believed they were the producers of all wealth and resented the merchants, who took some of this wealth for themselves (Azevedo, 1958, pp. 105–22). This conflict was exacerbated by the issue of "nationality": the Brazilian-born senhores felt that they were "sons of the soil," and that the crown discriminated in favor of the primarily Portuguese-born merchants, whom the planters disparagingly called *mascates* ("peddlers") or *marinheiros* ("sailors") (Prado, p. 345). The fluctuation of sugar prices, seasonality of purchasing power, and the high prices of slaves and other imported goods led the planters and mill owners into debt while the merchants attained a life-style that rivaled theirs in conspicuous consumption—and, being urban, was even more conspicuous. Nevertheless, the crown did support the interests of the senhores at the expense of the creditors by prohibiting seizure of lands and slaves for unpaid debts (Azevedo, 1958, pp. 144–45).

In 1710, the conflicts between the senhores de engenho and the Pernambuco merchants exploded into an armed confrontation. Olinda, then the capital of Pernambuco, was the senhores' base of power, and they resented attempts by the merchants to raise nearby Recife, already much larger than Olinda, to the status of an independent villa. The senhores and their supporters invaded Recife, were expelled, and then laid siege to the city until a new governor arrived from Portugal. The governor supported the Recife merchants and imprisoned some of the senhores who had led the revolt (see Ibarguen). Although the sugar aristocracy continued to play the major role in the political, economic, and social life of the region, the merchants had carved out their own niche in the colonial political structure.

The growing prestige of the cities was an important factor in the increasing absenteeism of the senhores de engenho. While early travelers had noted that the *casa grande* of the engenho was the center of Brazilian social life, by 1800 many landowners were spending most of the year in the cities. According to Prado, by the end of the colonial era,

> even in the colony's largest centers the population of rural origin continued to predominate, if not in numbers, at least in prestige and wealth. The cream of society in the large centers was drawn from the fazendeiros, the senhores d'engenho and the wealthy copyholders. They lived on their fazendas and engenhos during the busiest season, or at harvest time—if they were very conscientious, which was not always the case—but for the rest of the year they preferred the pleasures and diversifications of the city. Absenteeism was the rule among the big landed proprietors, and this fact was deplored by all who wanted to see an improvement in agricultural production, usually left to negligent or incompetent managers. [P. 342]

This chapter has been primarily concerned with the power relationships between the senhores de engenho and the other classes and the formation of control mechanisms that operated in favor of the landowners, but there were other aspects of Brazil's institutional development which—while less directly related to the issue of economic control—had an influence that persists to the present day. One is the relationship of race and class to each other and to attitudes toward work. Another is the Brazilian educational system; lack of support for education has colonial origins, yet continues to undermine development efforts in Brazil's Northeast. Dietary patterns are another: they were formed in the colonial era to meet the needs of sugar monoculture, but continue today.

Three studies of racial attitudes in rural Brazil found that *negros* (a term which does not correspond to its counterpart in English) are regarded as the best workers, although other races are regarded as most intelligent, most honest, most religious, most attractive, etc. (H. W. Hutchinson, p. 36; Harris, p. 58; Zimmerman, p. 99). Harris remarks that this does not indicate any conflict within racial stereotypes, "since the capacity to do the type of work implied, namely heavy physical labor, is scarcely something to be admired" (p. 54). This attitude toward labor is the natural heritage of a slave society and of a postslavery society in which the wages of a manual laborer are barely adequate to meet minimum physiological needs, and where the workers see a definite inverse relationship between the amount of physical labor and the level of living.

Efforts to modernize the Brazilian Northeast will come into conflict with these attitudes toward work and race. Cuban leaders found the attitude of the peasantry toward manual labor to be a serious barrier to development.

The Cuban Revolution, according to Huberman and Sweezy, was

> unavoidably destroying the entire system of pressures which for cen-
> turies had driven the Cuban peasantry to work. At bottom this system
> was based on one thing and on one thing only: fear of starvation. The
> peasant worked as much and as hard as he could because that was the
> only way to get food for himself and his family. After the Revolution
> he could feed his family much better while working much less, and
> the state threw in for good measure things he might have longed for
> but never enjoyed. All his traditional, one might say inborn, reasons
> for working hard disappeared. Unless new reasons could be substi-
> tuted, the most natural and human thing in the world was for him to
> stop working any harder than required to enjoy his new and much
> higher standard of life. [P. 144]

The pathetic state of education in northeastern Brazil is also a result of
four centuries of sugarcane monoculture. An article by Douglass North
shows how a plantation economy can retard educational development. He
compares two hypothetical regions, one in which the export product can be
produced efficiently on family farms, and the other in which the export
product has extreme economies of scale. The region with family farms will
have a relatively equitable distribution of income, new industries will develop to serve the residents of the region, and the residents will take an active interest in their region's development and will support education and
research. But the region that produces the plantation commodity will have
little opportunity to diversify, and a lack of educational interest is a key
link in this retardation process:

> Under the plantation type with very unequal income distribution, the
> planter will be extremely reluctant to devote his tax monies to ex-
> penditure for education or research other than that related to the
> staple commodity. As a consequence skills and knowledge not di-
> rectly related to the export commodity will be at a low level. In con-
> trast, the region with more equitable income distribution will be well
> aware of the stake in improving its comparative advantage through
> education and research and will accordingly be willing to devote pub-
> lic expenditure in these directions. The result will be to improve its
> comparative position in a variety of types of economic activity and
> therefore broaden the resultant economic base. [P. 72]

Nineteenth-century Brazil saw the founding and failure of many trade
and agricultural schools, while law and professional school enrollment continued to climb:

The Imperial Instituto Fluminense de Agricultura and other similar institutes which were founded in Bahia, Pernambuco, Sergipe, and Rio Grande,—associations created with the object of spreading, theoretically and practically, the best systems of agriculture and of exploitation of the land—, did not merely not succeed in accomplishing a useful and lasting work, but not even in rising from the swamp in which they were stagnating in apathetic and almost indifferent government. This picture, which is really discouraging, . . . showed in its neglect for popular and professional education the dominant literary and rhetorical mentality as well as the slave-owning spirit, which was opposed or showed itself indifferent to every effort to direct general education in the direction of social and economic conditions or with more practical and utilitarian objects. The work of the land, like mechanical and industrial activity, seemed reserved to the ignorant and incapable and was hardly to be adjusted to that kind of nobility which passage through school conferred,—passage through secondary schools and the higher faculties destined to train for the liberal professions. [Azevedo, 1950, p. 383]

Another distressing and, unfortunately, lasting aspect of sugarcane monoculture has been its effect on dietary habits. The first Portuguese to settle in the Northeast discovered a rich land, replete with fruit and wildlife and capable of producing most of the foodstuffs to which the Portuguese had become accustomed during the period of Moslem domination. The indigenous population had a highly varied food culture, and the slaves imported from Africa had a varied and balanced food culture of their own, including high-vitamin-content sauces made from tropical plants. But the colonists' single-minded concentration on sugar production eliminated this variety and put in its place a monotonous diet of manioc flour and beans. Manioc became the mainstay of the slave's diet. Large quantities could be grown in small areas and with little labor, making few demands on the senhor do engenho's labor force. The slaves were able to reestablish their previous rich diets only when they escaped into the backlands. Soldiers who conquered the Republic of Palmares reported seeing a great variety of cultivated plants (Castro, 1965, pp. 107–21).

The poor of the Northeast today have an incredible number of taboos about local fruits and other foods. The fruits could provide a rich source of many needed vitamins; for example, mangoes, rich in vitamin A, are usually abundant and cheap, yet a regional nutrition survey indicated exceptionally low vitamin A consumption (ICNND, p. 98). Josué de Castro lists some of the taboos still prevalent among the northeastern peasants and postulates their origin: "By asserting so as to make the slaves—and later the moradores—believe that no fruit should be mixed with alcohol, that watermelon eaten shortly after being picked causes fever, that mango eaten with milk is poison, that oranges can only be eaten early in the morning, that fruit a little overripe gives cramps, that sugarcane causes diarrhea, the senhores and bosses extremely diminished the possibilities that the poor would go so far as to touch the fruits that they were selfishly hoarding for their own exclusive use" (1965, p. 135; my translation). These traditional prohibitions are supplemented by a general policy of engenhos and usinas against allowing employees to plant trees on the land surrounding their houses. The landowners fear that the employees may establish some legal claim to tenure under future laws (CIDA, p. 235).

Although the land-owning class was directly responsible for the early institutional formation of northeastern Brazil, the sugar barons have not retained their once total control over national and regional institutions. However, the new groups that have come to share power—the industrial and commercial bourgeoisie, the government and industry technicians, and the military—find their options severely limited through the institutional results of four centuries of monoculture. Gambs writes that institutions "tend to give a semi-permanent coercive advantage to certain groups at the expense of others" (p. 22). Northeastern Brazil's sugar industry is outmoded—neither being economically capable of surviving in a laissez-faire environment nor contributing to the region's social or economic welfare. Its present survival stems largely from institutions generated in the past.

5. The Abolition of Slavery and the Evolution of Free Labor

Freeing the Negro without freeing the land is but half an abolition.

Joaquim Nabuco

Social, economic, and political changes converged to eliminate slavery from Brazil in the nineteenth century. Importation of slaves was effectively prohibited in 1850. In 1871, the Law of Free Birth was passed, freeing all slaves born after its passage and either giving the slave owner a cash indemnification if he released the slave at the age of eight, or allowing him to keep the slave (now legally an ''apprentice'') until his twenty-first birthday and then free him without compensation. In 1885, the Law of Sexagenarians, passed by Parliament after an earlier defeat, declared all slaves free on their sixtieth birthday. In May 1888, while the emperor was in Europe, Princess Isabel formed a new cabinet under the leadership of a Pernambuco Conservative and asked Parliament to abolish slavery without compensation to the slave owners. This legislation, called the Golden Law, passed with tremendous majorities through a Parliament that generally represented the interests of the landowners (Haring, pp. 83–106).

The ease with which slavery was abolished is indicative of the changes in Brazil's economic and political structure that occurred in the nineteenth century. There was no armed struggle as in the United States, nor was abolition forced by an outside power as in the British West Indies. There were few economic repercussions, and the political impact is difficult to determine. Nor were the slaves themselves greatly affected by abolition.

Less than two years after abolition, the armed forces deposed Emperor

Dom Pedro II in a bloodless coup and proclaimed a republic. Although abolition had helped to undermine the emperor's support, it was only one of many causes of change in the system of government. The Northeast's sugar industry had been reducing its dependence on slavery throughout the latter half of the century. Changes in technology and world market conditions, not the abolition, caused the industry's decline in the last two decades of the century.

The first step toward emancipation—stopping the flow of new slaves from Africa—came at a time when the demand for slave labor was increasing. Sugar exports were up, cotton was becoming a major northeastern crop and was drawing many free laborers from the coast, and coffee production—initially based on slavery—was rapidly expanding in the Paraíba Valley in the province of Rio de Janeiro. While the emperor favored abolition, most groups influencing national policy were opposed to stopping the slave trade. That the importation of slaves was outlawed as early as 1850 was primarily a result of Britain's efforts to stop the trade throughout the world.

Britain had enjoyed a special relationship with the Portuguese since the seventeenth century, receiving special commercial privileges in Portugal in exchange for military aid. The English fleet helped the Portuguese court—fleeing from the French—escape to Brazil in 1807, and England's commercial privileges were thereby transferred to Brazil. When Brazil declared independence in 1822, the new nation sought recognition by established European powers. In 1827, Brazil signed a treaty with England agreeing to abolish the slave trade within three years; this, along with a tariff agreement favorable to English manufacturers, was the price of England's recognition. However, Brazilians continued to import slaves in violation of the treaty. British enforcement was hampered by the lack of an "equipment clause": only the actual presence of slaves on board the ship was accepted as evidence of slave trading. Slavers chased by British ships threw slaves overboard to escape prosecution (Manchester, p. 226).

By the 1840s, Britain's patience with Brazil's evasion of the treaty was clearly exhausted. In 1845, Parliament passed the Aberdeen Bill, authorizing British cruisers to capture Brazilian slavers and try them for piracy in British courts. Ninety Brazilian ships were seized between August 1849, and May 1852, some of them in Brazilian ports and rivers. By 1850, Dom Pedro II—whose sympathies were clearly abolitionist—had consolidated and centralized his power to the point that he could ignore regionalist pressures. An antinationalist revolt in Pernambuco had been put down in 1848 with a consequent loss of Liberal power. In addition, many Conservative

politicians believed that Brazil could only maintain sovereignty by outlaw-
ing the slave trade and enforcing the law in Brazilian courts. The law
abolishing the trade was passed in September 1850 and relentlessly executed. Fifty-four thousand slaves had been imported in 1849; by 1852
fewer than 700 were brought in, and there were no known slave landings
after 1856 (Manchester, pp. 254–65).

British rhetoric would have us believe that their efforts to stop the trade
sprung from humanitarian sentiment and Christian consideration, but Britain's economic self-interest was visible not far below the surface. By
1806, 6,000 tons of West Indies sugar had accumulated in British warehouses (Williams, p. 149). Abolishing the slave trade would prevent Brazil
and Cuba, both of which had unused land suitable for cane, from increasing their production to compete with West Indies sugar in the European
markets. In the British West Indies, almost all of the available land was
being used and cane plantings could not be expanded. Even though prefer-
ential tariffs guaranteed the home market to West Indies sugar producers,
Britain had to reexport West Indies sugar to Europe to avoid accumulating
surpluses. But Britain could not refuse to purchase Brazilian sugar without
losing Brazil as a market for manufactured goods. British industrial interests campaigned for free trade in sugar—British merchant ships were returning from Brazil empty, and the merchants wanted to purchase more
Brazilian sugar (Williams, pp. 155–57; Manchester, pp. 166–67). Within
the limitations imposed by colonial and domestic politics, Parliament's
course was clear: for the West Indian sugar producers—abolish the slave
trade; for the British manufacturers and shippers—abolish the differential
sugar tariff. One was accomplished in the name of human rights and the
other was heralded as the triumph of the natural economic law of free trade.

The slave trade was stopped just as more labor was needed for a new export crop. Coffee had begun to be exported in appreciable quantities at the
end of the eighteenth century, when the Haitian revolution disrupted one of
the world's major coffee sources. By 1830, coffee accounted for 18 percent
of the value of Brazilian exports and was third on the export list, after sugar
and cotton. By mid-century, coffee—now the major export—earned 40
percent of Brazil's export income (Furtado, 1963, p. 123). Brazil's economic center was shifting from the Northeast to the southern provinces of
Rio de Janeiro and São Paulo. Even the slave labor force was shifting to the
South. The sugar states of the Northeast tried to stop slave sales to the
South—as well as to raise revenue—by taxing slave exports. In 1859 Pernambuco's export tax was 200 mil-réis per slave—equivalent in value to
the wages that a free agricultural laborer could earn in eight months. In

1862, the slave tax was Alagoas's major source of revenue (da Costa, pp. 156, 177). In spite of the tax, the number of slaves in the Northeast declined. In 1823 there were almost 500,000 slaves in Bahia, Pernambuco, and Maranhão, and less than 400,000 in Rio de Janeiro, São Paulo, and Minas Gerais; by 1873 the three northeastern states had fewer than 350,000 slaves and the three southern states had nearly 800,000 (da Costa, p. 156).

With the cessation of slave importations and the new demand for labor in the coffee sector, the price of slaves increased rapidly. The perfectly elastic labor supply enjoyed by the sugar industry during its period of expansion was not available to the coffee planters. Slaves that would have sold for 1,000 mil-réis in 1855 cost from 2,500 to 3,000 mil-réis in 1875 (da Costa, p. 155). But it was not prices alone that led many coffee planters to hire free laborers. Coffee required a greater ground area than sugar and this made close supervision expensive. Many coffee planters hoped to attract European immigrants and realized that Europeans would not readily immigrate to a country that still practiced slavery (da Costa, p. 178). Thus, many southern coffee planters joined the campaign for abolition, at the same time that their growing power was destroying the near-monopoly of public power that had sustained the northeastern senhores de engenho for so many centuries.

Brazilian industrial development added another new class who found slavery opposed to their economic interest. The industrialists, like the coffee planters, did not want to tie up capital in the purchase of a labor force. Nor did they want to concern themselves with feeding, housing, and clothing a labor force. As Mandel points out, slavery's relationship to capitalism has always been contradictory:

> The special relations which, by the creation of the industrial reserve army and by the economic role of ground rent, link agriculture with industry in the capitalist epoch, gave rise to the special forms of development in agriculture itself. The introduction of slavery in the American colonies between the sixteenth and nineteenth centuries, the introduction of forced labour in the African and Oceanian colonies at the end of the nineteenth and in the twentieth century were, in the special conditions of the countries in question, necessary conditions for creating *capitalist property-relations* in these countries. They none the less hindered for a long time the penetration of *capitalist production-relations* in the country. [P. 288; italics Mandel's]

Railroads pushed across the São Paulo plateau, telegraph lines linked the country, and small industries grew to meet increasing domestic demand.

While there had been only nine cotton mills in Brazil in 1866 (five of them in Bahia), by 1885 there were forty-eight, most of them in the Central-South (Stein, p. 21). By 1860, Brazil's tariff rate was 50 percent; imported textiles were taxed at a 60 percent rate (Leff, p. 9).

While economic forces operated to hasten emancipation, abolitionist propaganda generated its own economic effects. A new urban class of technicians, government functionaries, and military officers was forming. Most segments of this class were opposed to slavery on humanistic and philosophical grounds. By the 1880s people in the cities were openly protecting escaped slaves. With public opinion mounting on the side of emancipation, the army became reluctant to hunt runaways and return them to their masters. Escapes became increasingly commonplace, and railway employees openly aided slaves trying to get to the cities. Graham notes that the slave owners began to favor abolition as a means of keeping the slaves on the plantations. To the slave, the concept of freedom was apparently more social than economic; he would escape to the city to obtain "freedom," yet remain on the sugar plantation or coffee *fazenda* if "freedom" were granted by the owner. Many planters regarded the final abolition of slavery as little more than the legalization of a fait accompli (Graham, p. 124).

Throughout the nineteenth century, free labor became more important in the sugar economy. Henry Koster, an Englishman who managed two Pernambuco sugar plantations around 1810, reported widespread use of free workers in the cane fields (pp. 118–31). Many senhores de engenho preferred free laborers for those jobs whose dangerous or particularly exhausting nature would endanger the life or health of a valuable slave (Koster, p. 166). As early at 1855, almost half of the sugarcane in Pernambuco was produced by free laborers (Andrade, p. 96).

The increased use of free workers was made possible by a growing population and the latifundia's monopoly of the land. A 1774 census indicated that the entire Northeast was populated, and that the engenhos monopolized the land as far inland as Vitória de Santo Antão, the present limit of cane cultivation in Pernambuco (Andrade, p. 71). Population growth was rapid. The population of Paraíba more than tripled from 122,407 in 1825 to 377,226 in 1872. Free population accounted for practically the entire increase, as the number of slaves increased only by about 1,500 (Andrade, p. 96). Several factors limited the industry's labor needs in the latter half of the century. Brazil was not benefiting from the growth of sugar consumption in the United States and Europe; Cuba was expanding production to meet the needs of the United States, and the autarkical economic policies of many European nations led to dependence on domestically produced beet sugar. The increase in northeastern sugar production that did take place in the last two decades was due to the installation of steam mills and central sugar factories, rather than to extension of the cane fields. A modern usina obtained almost twice as much sugar from a given amount of cane as an animal- or water-driven mill.

Those opposed to abolition had predicted that emancipation would be disastrous for Brazil. The slave was part of the capital stock of the nation, and freeing him would destroy this wealth forever. Furtado underlines the fallacy of this argument:

> Abolition of slavery, like agrarian reform, does not imply per se either destruction or creation of wealth. What it does amount to is merely a redistribution of property within a community. The apparent complexity of the problem arises from the fact that property rights over the working force, when passing from the slave master to the individual laborer himself, cease being an *asset* included in bookkeeping entries and become a mere potentiality. From the economic point of view, the fundamental aspect of the problem lies in the repercussions of the redistribution of property on the organization of production, as well as on the utilization of available factors and distribution and final utilization of the income created. [1963, p. 149]

Furtado's comments indicate the significance of the statement by Joaquim Nabuco, the Pernambuco abolitionist quoted in the epigraph at the beginning of this chapter. In an agrarian society, labor and land are the major factors of production, and no production is possible with either land or labor by itself. Wealth is usually regarded as income-earning capacity: the slave was a capital good, whose purchaser could expect to realize a stream of income from the investment. Land is wealth in the same sense. If we consider income distribution instead of wealth distribution, we see that emancipation without land reform would have no effect at all. After 1888 the slave "owned" himself, yet his "wealth" did not entitle him to the same stream of income the senhor do engenho had enjoyed, as the senhor still retained the other factor of production—the land. Since the former slave's only option was starvation, he had to continue living as he had before emancipation: working for the senhor and earning the bare necessities for survival. Here we have the apparent paradox of a major portion of the senhor's capital stock being taken from him without reducing his income.

The abolition of slavery in Jamaica is an example of the opposite situation. England ordered the slaves freed before the Jamaican sugar planters and others in the land-owning class had gained control over most of the colony's central highlands. The slaves left the coastal sugar plantations to farm previously unused land. The Jamaican sugar planters tried to retain their labor force by encouraging European immigrants to fill the central highlands and force the former slaves back to the plantations (Hall, p. 21). The same situation occurred in Brazil's northeastern state of Maranhão. The sugar industry in Maranhão was relatively new at the time of abolition, and there were still large tracts of uninhabited land. The Maranhão sugar industry was virtually destroyed by emancipation (see Pinheiro).

For several reasons, the sugar producers of the Northeast were able to retain their labor force, even while the South was importing laborers from Europe. The senhores de engenho attenuated the mobility of their workers by lending them small amounts of cash or selling them foodstuffs and other necessities on credit. The worker could not leave until he had liquidated the debt, and his low income made this difficult (Andrade, p. 94). Also, it is doubtful that the ex-slaves knew of the opportunities in the coffee regions of São Paulo. Their only source of information would have been by word of mouth; it is unlikely that any senhor would have allowed labor recruiters to operate on his property. Moreover, few ex-slaves could have accumulated enough money to make the arduous journey. Finally, always having lived in a condition of servitude made it very unlikely that the former slave would travel almost 2,000 miles to search for higher-paying employment. The system of economic incentives is generally unknown to the person raised as a slave (Furtado, 1963, p. 153).

While the living standard of the former slave did not change, his leisure time did increase. This was not related to the abolition of slavery as much as to the decreased demand for labor resulting from population increases and a practically stagnant sugar market. The slave of the seventeenth and eighteenth centuries worked in the cane fields or mill six days a week, and used the one remaining day to produce his own foodstuffs. The new economic and demographic conditions of the latter part of the nineteenth century diminished the amount of labor that the senhor could utilize from each laborer. The former slave became a morador. As before, he produced his own foodstuffs. In return for the land he was allowed to use, he agreed to work two or three days per week for the senhor, for either no pay or an extremely low—almost nominal—wage. This system was known as *condição*, or *cambão* (literally, "ox-yoke"). Whereas the senhor previously had been able to extract the surplus product from the laborer by virtue of his ownership of the laborer, he now did essentially the same thing by virtue of his ownership of the land. The major difference to the laborer was that the surplus he was forced to produce had diminished. The increased population enabled the senhor to have more people on his property, thus increasing his political power and prestige.

Two distinct economic systems arose in the zona da mata. The engenhos on the fringes of the mata—those, for example, in Vitória de Santo Antão and Bonita in Pernambuco—were bypassed by the large usinas that came to dominate the cane fields by the first decade of the twentieth century. The engenhos could neither produce sugar competitively in their primitive mills nor sell cane to the usinas. The moradores on these engenhos no longer had to plant cane; they raised what they pleased and paid a cash rent to the landowner. Their living standard increased and the local markets became famous for an abundance of fruits and vegetables (Andrade, p. 109). The land closer to the coast, most of it owned by the usinas, remained in cane, and the usinas kept most of the field workers on the cambão. In some areas, this system continued into the 1960s. As late as 1962, field workers on the plantations owned by Usina Miriri in Paraíba were receiving one-half hectare plots of land for an unpaid cambão of one day per week. Even at the low prevailing wage rates and inflated land values of that period, two years (100 days) of such labor were equal in value to the small plots of land the peasants used (Andrade, p. 254).

The labor compensation system that replaced slavery on the engenhos of the Northeast is often described as feudal. The cambão has the appearance of feudalism: the peasant trades labor to the landowner for a plot of land on which he raises food to feed his family. However, it is important to understand the differences between the cambão, as it was practiced in the zona da mata of northeastern Brazil, and true feudalism. Feudalism implies that the relationship between the land, the landowner, and the peasant is somehow noneconomic, that it is based on tradition rather than on the profit motive, and that the landowner who is following his economic self-interest can alter his system of production and increase his profit.

European feudalism was a result of the decline of the trading relationships that had existed in the Roman Empire when agriculture was based on slave labor and had attained a high level of technological sophistication. When the Roman Empire dissolved, specialization based on trade could not continue, as the trade routes were no longer policed and the order necessary for commerce had disappeared. But the technology with its consequent high levels of potential production remained. As most food products were perishable, there was little point in producing a surplus; and the pace of agricultural labor became more relaxed than it had been when trading possibilities had existed. Over a period of several centuries, traditions developed defining the responsibilities and privileges of each class (Furtado, 1967, pp. 89–92). The power of even the feudal lord was circumscribed by tradition. The traditions created a highly stable society which took several centuries to dissolve, even after possibilities of trade and increased production through specialization were resumed in the mercantile era.

The senhor do engenho, however, did not abandon market production or specialization when slavery ended. As he had abundant unused land, the cambão was the cheapest way to obtain a labor force. Having a large number of moradores on his property assured him of adequate labor in peak seasons. To attempt to squeeze more work from his moradores would involve costly administration and overseeing. He had no commitment to the cambão as a traditional system; when economic forces later made abandoning the cambão and replacing it with a wage system profitable, he readily adapted to the new conditions.

6. The Usinas

There was no doubt that they wanted to speed up the sale of the Santa Rosa plantation. Now they would not give me the price the plantation was worth. In this tight spot, with a noose around my neck, I would accept any offer. Seventy thousand *mil-réis*, not including the interest—they would make me the worst possible offer in the world. Two square miles of land, forests, first-class water practically on the plantation, valley, hills, enormous pasture lands, machinery of the finest quality—all that they would get for nothing.

José Lins do Rêgo

At the beginning of the nineteenth century, there was little that distinguished Brazilian sugar-production methods from those of the early 1600s. The cane varieties; the method of cultivation; the vertical milling apparatus driven by horses, oxen, or water; the evaporation in shallow pans over brick ovens; the formation of sugar loaves in clay forms; and the furnaces that consumed oxcart upon oxcart of wood had not changed in 200 years. By the end of the nineteenth century, however, Brazil's sugar industry had undergone a radical transformation. Slavery was gone. The domestic market had passed the international market in importance: 70 percent of the 1901 crop was for domestic consumption (Andrade, p. 100). The usinas were spreading their lifelines, the narrow-gauge private railroads, throughout the cane fields. The old engenhos were becoming cane plantations, shutting down their mills and selling cane to the usinas. A tradition of two centuries of subdivision of the original land grants reversed itself as both land and capital came to be concentrated in the hands of the usineiros.

The senhores de engenho started using new cane varieties in the early 1800s. *Caiana*, brought from French Guiana, was widely used until it be-

67

came susceptible to several diseases. New varieties of caiana—*imperial* and *cristalina*—gained wide acceptance. Some senhores conducted their own cane-breeding experiments. *Manteiga*, a popular variety which replaced imperial and cristalina toward the end of the nineteenth century, was developed through selection and crossbreeding by Manuel Cavalcanti de Albuquerque at his engenho in Vitória de Santo Antão, Pernambuco (Andrade, p. 85).

The need for modern processing methods became apparent in the late nineteenth century. The traditional mills were only obtaining 4.5–6 kilograms of sugar per 100 kilograms of cane (da Costa, p. 170). This was low-quality sugar, no longer acceptable on the international market (Andrade, pp. 98–99). As early as 1853, 14 percent of the world's sugar was produced from beets (DNP, p. 37). Beet sugar was produced in modern European plants and was of much better quality than the sugar produced in Brazil's primitive mills. In the 1870s, Cuban sugar production began to be dominated by the large *centrales*, modern mills producing as much as 10 kilograms of sugar per 100 kilograms of cane. They used vacuum pans and centrifuges, whereas the Brazilian engenhos used open pots. Only with modern equipment could Brazil produce sugar pure enough to bring a high price on the international market.

The first stage of mechanization was the replacement of animal- and water-driven mills by steam mills. The first steam mill in Brazil was installed in Bahia in 1815 (da Costa, p. 170), another in Pernambuco in 1819 (Andrade, p. 86). Steam mills were expensive and their acceptance was slow. In 1857 only 18 of the 1,106 sugar mills in Pernambuco were steam-driven, while 346 were water-driven and the remainder were powered by animals (da Costa, p. 170). A factory in Recife attempted to manufacture steam mills, and a Brazilian-made mill was completed in 1836; but a treaty with England prevented Brazil from giving tariff protection to the nascent industry, and the factory did not survive (da Costa, p. 170). Perhaps the most important technical change in this period was the introduction of bagasse (a fibrous waste product from the cane) as a fuel. Many engenhos had been closed due to wood shortages, so this practice spread rapidly (Andrade, p. 87).

The second stage of modernization—the introduction of large central mills—began in the 1870s. Foreign loans for the construction of these *engenhos centrais* were guaranteed by a law of 1875. They were to be modern sugar factories, producing white sugar with steam mills and the most advanced centrifuges and vacuum pans. Government policy makers hoped to ''rationalize'' sugar production by separating field operations from processing. Their charters prohibited the engenhos centrais from owning land and attempted to zone them to prevent competition for cane. Most centrais were installed and operated by foreign corporations. The senhores resisted the foreign mills, and there were many difficulties with cane-supplying contracts. Many central mills were only in operation for one year (da Costa, p. 172; Andrade, p. 87).

Although the engenhos centrais failed to revitalize the sugar industry, the usinas succeeded. The usinas were built on the lands of former engenhos, usually by the owner of the engenho. Many founders of usinas owned several engenhos in one location (Andrade, p. 99); thus they were guaranteed a supply of cane, whereas the central mills had depended on contracts. Often, the senhores de engenho in one area were related and would combine their resources to establish an usina. In 1891, José da Silva Cisneiros Guimarães, Manuel Cisneiros da Costa Reis, José Cisneiros de Albuquerque Melo, and Afonso Artur Cisneiros de Albuquerque—owners of the neighboring engenhos Utinga de Cima, Castelo, Olinda, and Bonfim—founded Costa Reis, Cisneiros & Cia. to build and operate the usina Maria das Mercês in Cabo, Pernambuco (Felipe, p. 177). A law passed in 1890 permitted usinas to acquire other engenhos and left the price of sugarcane to be determined by the usina and engenho concerned (Lima, 1941, p. 12). This permitted domination of cane lands by the usinas.

With exceptionally high sugar prices, the installation of usinas proceeded apace from 1890 to 1900. In the 1870s, sugar prices had fallen to less than two cruzieros per arroba. During most of the 1890s, crystal sugar sold for ten cruzieros per arroba. However, the high prices of that period stimulated growth of sugar industries in other nations, and in 1901 the price plunged to four cruzieros per arroba (Andrade, pp. 97–99). Beet sugar replaced cane sugar in many markets, accounting for 44 percent of world sugar production by the turn of the century (DNP, p. 43). But the new usinas rode out the crisis, and additional usinas were built even before sugar prices recovered during World War I (Andrade, p. 99). By 1920 there were 144 usinas in the Northeast. Seventy of these were small usinas in Sergipe, where each generally replaced one engenho (Andrade, p. 100).

After 1920, increases in capacity came about through the improvement and expansion of existing usinas, rather than through installation of new ones. Whereas there had been fifty-four of them in Pernambuco in 1920, there were only forty-four by 1968. The large mills ground increasing portions of the region's sugar. In 1955, Usina Catende in Pernambuco produced more sugar than all thirty-six usinas in the state of Sergipe (Andrade, p. 101). By 1965, over 50 percent of Pernambuco's sugar was processed by eleven of the state's forty-seven usinas (see IAA). The new technology drastically altered the minimum economic size of operation. Even the best of the water-driven mills of the previous century could not have produced more than 150,000 kilograms of sugar, yet the *smallest* usina in Pernambuco in 1965—since gone out of production—produced 1,080,000 kilograms, and eleven Pernambuco usinas each produced more than 24,000,000 kilograms.

The success of the usinas depended on efficient transportation. Cane's rapid spoilage rate limited the radius of any engenho. Deer calculates that cane loses 2.2 percent of its weight in 24 hours after cutting, 4 percent in 48 hours, 5.5 percent in 72 hours, and 7.4 percent in 96 hours. The amount of sugar that can be extracted from the cane decreases even more rapidly: 2.7 percent of the available sugar is lost within 24 hours; 8 percent within 48 hours; and 21.4 percent within 72 hours (Deer, 1911, p. 168). Mules and oxcarts transported cane at about two miles per hour, whereas the narrow-gauge railways installed by usinas averaged ten to twelve miles per hour (Deer, 1911, p. 161). Although railways were an expensive investment, the extension of the usina's operating radius made large usinas feasible. Railways also reduced the need to maintain the large pastures and labor forces that animal transportation required. Even a small usina might have as many as 65 kilometers of rail line. In 1966, there were 2,279.5 kilometers of usina-owned rail lines in Pernambuco (GERAN, p. 21).

Government policy makers' plans for "rational" sugar production, with separate ownership of field and factory, were soon shattered. Modern technology, which continually demands larger and larger scales of operation, and the capitalist system, which gives the largest and most successful producers an economic advantage over smaller producers, were not to be denied. Domination of the regional economy by large usinas was not unique to Brazil. Cuban economists of the 1860s also proposed the separation of planting and milling activities; but, in Cuba as in Brazil, policies and theories failed to stop the giant mills from controlling their sources of raw materials (Guerra y Sánchez, pp. 61–67). Nor was the drive to own the source of raw materials unique to the sugar industry, although it may have been more vital in sugar than in other industries; many economic reasons have traditionally led industries to seek such control: "Controlling raw materials sources is both a protective device against pressure of competitors as well as a weapon of offense to keep non-integrated competitors in line. Ownership of and control over raw material supplies is, as a rule, an essential prerequisite for the ability of a leading firm or group of leading firms to limit new competition and to control production and prices of the finished products'' (Magdoff, p. 35). It is not without reason that Andrade characterizes the usina as a "Dom João [imperialist] of lands'' (p. 101).

Ownership and / or control of the sources of raw materials are more important to sugar mills than to many other industries. The mill and its rail lines represent a considerable investment and will only return a profit when the capacity is fully utilized. Once the mill starts its seasonal operation, mill labor becomes a relatively fixed cost, and operating costs will not be reduced if there is no cane for several hours or days (Swerling and Timoshenko, p. 71). However, if cane builds up at the mill faster than it can be processed, it will spoil and less sugar can be produced per unit of cane. Thus, close coordination of field and factory operations is a necessity.

The charters of the engenhos centrais specified a zone of influence for each central, guaranteeing that no other mill would purchase cane from within the specified boundaries. No such control was attempted with the usinas, and they were often built close together and battled to get their rail lines onto the best engenhos. From 1890 until 1932, the price of sugarcane was set by mutual agreement between the usina and the engenho. The advantage was clearly with the usina. According to Swerling and Timoshenko, the extraordinary power of the mill is characteristic of sugar economics throughout the world:

> Large industrial plants came into rural settings where economic units were characteristically small. The *central* became the economic and social core of the entire community, to the point where the manufacturing enterprise was on a par with the constituted political authorities as an instrument of local government. This was not an environment in which relationships between growers and laborers, on the one hand, and the mill, on the other, might be expected to work well on a purely market basis. In nineteenth century United States, rural dissatisfaction over the farmer's bargaining weakness in dealing with private railroads was an important factor in the introduction of public-utility regulation. In cane regions, not only may the mill be the exclusive market for the grower's crop, but the local railroads themselves are frequently under mill ownership. [P. 71]

There was no set price for sugarcane. The usina dealt with each engenho separately. The engenhos close to the usina and without any opportunity to sell their cane elsewhere were invariably paid a low price, while those being fought over by several usinas received exceptionally high prices (Lima, 1941, p. 14). Once an usina dominated an engenho by laying rails through it, the usina could set the minimum price which would induce the former senhor do engenho, now transformed into a *fornecedor da cana* ("cane planter"), to produce sugarcane. If the usina wanted to purchase the property, it might set a price so low that the fornecedor could not meet his expenses and would be forced to sell. The usina generally purchased as much of the surrounding property as it could (up to a point, which is discussed below). Records of Usina Goiana in Pernambuco show that it had a stated policy of buying all available lands so as to decrease its dependence on the planters (T. L. Smith, p. 348). Cuban centrales used the same strategy of domination:

> From the moment a central was able to invade another's traditional supply area, rivalry between the two was inevitable. At first there was an increase in the amount of sugar offered the colono in exchange for grinding his cane and, until a few years ago, it was still possible to identify these competing zones by the higher number of arrobas of sugar that the farmer received from the central for his cane. In Havana, Matanzas, and Santa Clara, where there were many centrales and a public railroad promoting their rivalry, the colono was free to sell his cane to the highest bidder and was given more than seven arrobas of sugar for every hundred of cane. In Camagüey, Oriente, and parts of Pinar del Río, where there were no railroads, only four—or at the most, five and a half—were offered.
>
> Competition created a new problem for the centrales: how to guarantee that each would have enough cane for each zafra at the lowest possible cost. This could be accomplished through one of two means: by economic domination of the colono—reducing his independence and making him a vassal of the mill, bound by contract and prevented from freely selling his product—or by purchasing lands and administering them as cane farms or having them sharecropped or rented by colonos dependent on the mill. [Guerra y Sánchez, pp. 66–67]

Once the senhor do engenho shut down his primitive mill and became a fornecedor, he would never again grind his own cane. The low price he would get for inferior sugar, the low recovery of sugar from cane, and the difficulty of reassembling a labor force to operate the mill practically eliminated this alternative to the usina's low prices. Knowing this, many senhores refused to shut their mills and sell cane to the usina; these small mills coexisted with the usinas for nearly seventy years. It was not until the 1950s that the *bangües*, as the small mills were called, were completely eliminated from the landscape of the zona da mata (Andrade, p. 103).

Until late in the 1930s, it was never in the economic interest of the usina to purchase *all* of the plantations that supplied its cane. By owning and administering all of them, the usina would be taking on all of the risks of the cane planter (Lima, 1941, p. 15). Until 1936, the usina was under no obligation to purchase cane in any given year from its usual suppliers. By owning and managing enough land to produce from 40 to 70 percent of the cane that it needed, the usina was free to make marginal adjustments in production at the expense of the independent fornecedores; yet it would still run a diminished risk of cane prices being driven up by shortages. As late as 1936, usinas were purchasing the following percentages of their cane from fornecedores: Paraíba, 25.6; Pernambuco, 58.3; Alagoas, 47.6; and Bahia, 33.5 (Lima, 1941, pp. 29–30).

The senhores de engenho, a class that had controlled the Northeast for over 300 years, were being replaced by the usineiros. Reduced to the status of fornecedores, the cane planters used the remnants of their political power to put legal roadblocks in the path of the usinas and their insatiable consumption of the land. In 1930, with the coming to power of Getulio Vargas, the government began to intervene, and in 1932 the price of sugarcane was set by law. One purpose of this law was to protect the fornecedores by removing the pricing of sugarcane from the control of the usinas (Lima, 1941, pp. 17–18). In 1933 the Institute of Sugar and Alcohol (IAA) was formed to administer production quotas and regulate the relationships between the usinas and the fornecedores. Government intervention in the sugar economy became even more direct in 1936, with the establishment of quotas for each planting unit supplying cane to the usinas (Lima, 1941, pp. 20–21).

Neither of these policies had its intended effects. Concentration of land ownership continued. Barbosa Lima Sobrinho, president of the IAA from 1938 to 1946, believed that the laws actually gave the usinas more reasons to increase their landholdings (Lima, 1941). Many usinas in the Northeast radically decreased their dependence on fornecedores in the 1930s. Usina Catende, the largest usina in Pernambuco, and Usina Bulhões, a medium-size usina in the same state, purchased, respectively, 84 and 100 percent of their sugarcane from fornecedores in the 1929–30 crop year. Throughout the 1930s, both usinas increased their own cane plantings until, by 1940–41, both were purchasing only 15 percent of their cane from outside suppliers (Lima, 1941, pp. 27–28). The fixing of cane prices and the setting of quotas made land ownership more attractive to the usinas (Lima, 1941, pp. 27–39).

The Statute of Cane Cultivation was passed in 1941 to correct the deficiencies of the earlier laws and to stem the growth of the usina latifundia.

It made incremental increases in the quotas for each usina dependent on how much cane it purchased from fornecedores. Any usina producing more than 60 percent of its sugar from its own cane was to transfer some of its cane fields to fornecedores until at least 40 percent of the cane it milled was purchased from independent planters (Lima, 1941). However, as "fornecedor" was defined as a renter, as well as an owner, of cane lands, there was little to prevent further acquisition of land by the usinas. The law failed to alter the land ownership situation in the Northeast (W. Carneiro, p. 28); many usinas still continue to plant 80 percent or more of the cane that passes through their mills (*Anuário Açucareiro*, 1960–61).

The total area of agricultural land in Pernambuco's zona da mata is 1,355,154 hectares. By 1966, 517,295 hectares were owned by the usinas. An additional 20 percent of the remaining land was indirectly owned by them (e.g., by direct relatives of usineiro families). Forty-six usinas and their associates, about fifteen actual individuals, own 51 percent of the agricultural land of a subregion with a population of over two million (GE-RAN, p. 21). Usina Catende, Central Barreiros, and Usina Santa Teresinha each own more than 35,000 hectares, and the properties of each are composed of more than fifty former engenhos (Andrade, p. 102). Multiple ownership of usinas and their associated lands is also common. Many family corporations own two mills, and one Pernambuco group owns four. Twelve Pernambuco family corporations produce 64 percent of that state's sugar (W. Carneiro, p. 34).

Many of the more apparent reasons for usina ownership of land disappeared with the increasing regulation of usina / engenho contracts by the IAA. However, other reasons took their place. While the quota system guaranteed each mill a supply of cane in the short run, only land ownership would guarantee a supply in the long run. If unchecked, the future tendency will probably be toward more concentration of land ownership. Rising food prices can make alternative uses of land financially attractive to the independent landowner. An engenho that stops producing cane to plant food crops removes labor, as well as land, from the reach of the usina. The political reasons for land ownership by the usinas are also important. IAA control over the price of sugarcane established a precedent of far-reaching significance. It became obvious to the usineiros that the price of cane would now depend on the ability of the senhores de engenho to press their claims on all political and bureaucratic levels. Usina ownership of the engenhos limited the senhores' political power by diminishing their numbers, as well as by insuring that any gains from increased cane prices would revert to the usinas. Until 1967, the tax structure also contributed to concentration of land ownership. The sales tax, replaced by a value-added tax in 1967, was collected at every point of transfer and encouraged vertical integration.

Another form of concentration is the gradual disappearance of small usinas and the absorption of their land by the larger usinas (Andrade, pp. 46–47). Between 1960 and 1968, ten usinas closed in Pernambuco alone. However, technical factors limit the scale of operations of northeastern usinas. Figure 4 shows the relationship between size and efficiency in Pernambuco usinas. The industrial yield, measured in kilograms of sugar per metric ton of cane, is the best measure of efficiency available, since the sugarcane is the mill's major cost. With the prices set by the IAA for the Northeast's 1968–69 crop, one ton of sugarcane was equal in value to 57 kilograms of sugar (*Brasil Açucareiro*, September 1968, pp. 79–81). In 1964–65, the crop year of the data used in Figure 4, eight usinas had industrial yields of less than 87 kilograms per ton of cane (87 k / t). Thirty had yields of from 87 to 93 k / t, and eight had yields greater than 93 k / t. Of two mills with the same milling capacity, one obtaining a yield of 93 k / t would have an income net of cane purchases 20 percent higher than the income of an usina obtaining only 87 k / t. Average yields in the Pernambuco sugar industry increase with usina size until a capacity of from 325,000 to 475,000 bags of sugar per year is reached, then fall as size in-

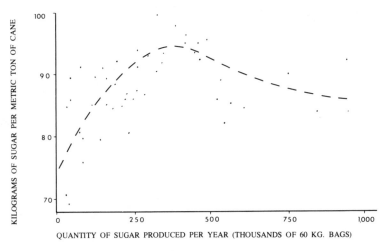

FIGURE 4. Relationship of size to efficiency in Pernambuco sugar mills. (Data from IAA, 1965.)

creases. No Pernambuco usina producing more than 475,000 bags per year obtains particularly high yields.

Survival of the small mills is endangered by two factors: the smaller output over which fixed operating costs can be spread, and the difficulty of obtaining high yields. Yet, the limitations to economies of scale seem to set a practical limit to the growth of the larger usinas. These limitations are probably caused by the difficulty of coordinating field and factory operations as size increases. They could be overcome by improving transportation and communications between the usina and the field operations. Availability of such improvements at a relatively low cost would give impetus to further consolidation. It would also be more efficient to increase the density of cane plantings on presently unused land close to the usinas, thereby reducing the distance that cane must be hauled; but this would conflict with other aspects of the political economy of sugar, to be discussed in chapter 8.

7. The Postwar Sugar Economy

The reentry of the Northeast into the world sugar market was not the result of an effective improvement in the competitive power of its product, but the result of the relative disorganization of this market caused by factors whose full implications are as yet unknown. The Northeastern sugar industry continues to have the lowest productivity of all the world's sugar exporting regions.

Celso Furtado

While the late nineteenth and early twentieth centuries were periods of rapid technological change in the sugar industry, the changes between the 1940s and the late 1960s—although of an entirely different nature—will have far-reaching significance for the future of northeastern Brazil. By the mid-1960s, the Northeast once again found itself tied to foreign demand for sugar. But it also found itself shut out of the domestic market by São Paulo's efficient sugar industry. Only a tenuous truce—a subsidy paid by the southern sugar industry to the northeastern producers—has kept the backward usinas and engenhos of that region from being swamped by São Paulo sugar. Yet sugar production in Pernambuco and Alagoas in the mid-1960s was nearly triple their prewar levels. And this increase in output was accompanied by another transformation of the labor system: the former morador now works for a daily wage.

Brazil's rapid industrialization and expanding per capita income in the 1940s and 1950s stimulated domestic demand for sugar. In the 1930s, annual per capita consumption of all types of sugar was about 25 kilograms; by the 1960s, consumption of centrifugal sugar alone was over 35 kilograms per person per year (see Figure 5). Demand was also stimulated by

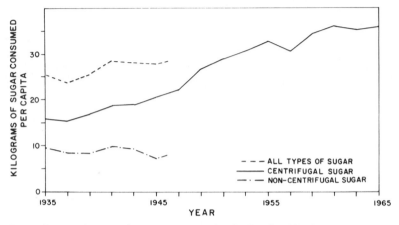

FIGURE 5. Annual per capita sugar consumption in Brazil, 1935–65. NOTE: Data on consumption of noncentrifugal sugar not collected after 1946. (Data from *Anuário Açucareiro*, various years.)

an expanding population; total consumption of centrifugal sugar tripled between 1940 and 1960 (see Figure 6). Yet, like the increasing incomes, the increasing sugar consumption was subject to immense regional disparities. Southern Brazil reached a per capita consumption level of 45.5 kilograms per year in the mid-1950s. This is near or above the consumption level in developed countries, and it is expected that further increases in this region will not exceed population growth. The Northeast, however, with an annual per capita sugar consumption level of 17.6 kilograms, had the lowest consumption of any of Brazil's regions (GERAN, p. 17). While this understates Northeasterners' sugar consumption by leaving out noncentrifugal sugars, it does indicate the limited regional market available to the Northeast's usinas.

Thus, Brazil's traditional sugar region found itself located far from the centers of sugar consumption. Moreover, these centers of consumption were able to become centers of production—the South's flat land is more adaptable to mechanization than Pernambuco's hilly cane fields. Southern sugar producers were prevented from meeting the southern demand only through the system of production controls established in the 1930s. It was the northeastern producer's political power, not a comparative advantage in cane farming and processing, that guaranteed him a place in the southern market. Even though São Paulo was the third largest sugar-producing state in Brazil by the mid-1930s, the São Paulo producers were only one pressure group among many in their state, whereas the Pernambuco and

Alagoas producers were the major economic interest groups in theirs. Leff describes a "threshold effect" wherein the concentration of Brazil's industry in São Paulo caused the agricultural interests of that state, including the coffee planters, to lose much of their political power early in the twentieth century (Leff, p. 28). Political divisions, then, can determine which groups will best be able to make their pressure felt at the national level. Unlike the São Paulo mill owners, Pernambuco usineiros—the Sampaio, Morais, and Queiroz families, for example—were consistently able to put their own members in the Pernambuco statehouse and federal congress. In 1965, every one of Pernambuco's twenty-nine usineiro families had a close relative or family member in *both* the federal congress and the Pernambuco assembly (Pearson, p. 21).

Their political power notwithstanding, the northeastern sugar producers were virtually excluded from the southern market by the 1960s. One factor leading to their exclusion was the way they used this power. Conditioned to the limited expectations of a stagnant economy, the northeastern usineiros were primarily interested in a price structure that would give them the best possible return on their investment. Their family corporations concentrated corporate power in the hands of one or two individuals or family members who held the top-level management positions in their usinas (Rosa e Silva,

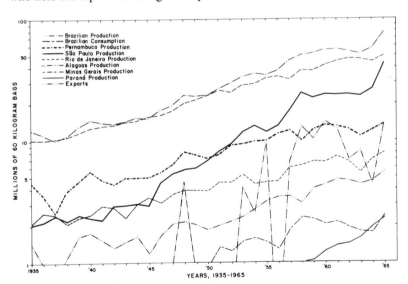

FIGURE 6. Brazilian production, consumption, and exports of centrifugal sugar and production by major states, 1935–65. NOTE: Semilogarithmic scale. (Data from *Anuário Açucareiro*, various years.)

pp. 130–31). There was little interest in expanding production beyond what could be managed by the family itself, and profits were generally used to purchase more land or to maintain their social and political status through lavish expenditure on luxuries and on political campaigns for family members. Ownership of the São Paulo sugar corporations was more fragmented and gave a professional class of managers more power over investment decisions. The São Paulo usineiros operated in a framework of rapid economic growth, with expectation of continued growth. Their interests were directed toward expansion.

World War II was the turning point in the growth of São Paulo and the Central-South as sugar producers. The war strained the Brazilian coastal shipping system, and overland transportation was too expensive for bulk commodities. Brazil's coastal fleet was old and outmoded, and the difficulty of obtaining parts restricted the available tonnage. Brazilian ships became targets for German torpedoes, and the convoys required for safety further slowed sugar transportation (Joint Commission, p. 85). Sugar was scarce in the South by 1943, even though there were more than 4,400,000 bags stored in northeastern warehouses. The IAA relaxed the enforcement of quotas in the Central-South, and this region surpassed its quotas by 1,454,314 sacks in 1941–42 and by 1,429,821 sacks in 1942–43. Only adverse weather conditions prevented the quotas from being surpassed by even greater amounts. The IAA, afraid that cutbacks in sugar purchases would destroy the Northeast's economic base and turn the sugar states into "centers of agitation," continued to purchase the unmarketable sugar and pile it up in northeastern warehouses (Lima, 1943).

The IAA tried to cope with the temporary wartime sugar shortage by permitting southern sugar production to increase without permanently damaging the Northeast's economic position. The law was revised to allow small mills, producing up to 400 sacks per year, to be established with a simple licensing procedure. However, firms or individuals who hoped to establish usinas at a later date would purchase eight small-mill licenses; once a company held licenses for 3,000 sacks per year, it could be recognized as an usina (see Oliveira). Although sugar production was ostensibly controlled through individual quotas, the usina that surpassed its quota was always able to sell its surplus to the IAA at a price close to the quota price. The operative control mechanism was provided by the difficulty of establishing a new usina and getting any quota, however small, permitting the production and sale of sugar. Thus, a program designed to meet a temporary crisis through the formation of small units with no growth potential backfired into providing the legal basis for the growth of the São Paulo sugar industry. Sugar producers in that state got another boost in 1946, when the IAA recognized sugar *consumption* in each state as a criterion for proportioning incremental increases in quotas among the states (Carli, pp. 102–3).

The postwar international sugar market allowed the Northeast to be "painlessly" displaced from its traditional markets. Whereas the Central-South had been the major market in the 1930s, by the mid-1950s the Northeast was selling most of its sugar abroad (see Figure 7). Although sugar production in Pernambuco and Alagoas more than doubled between 1945 and 1955, sugar sales to the Central-South remained constant during those years and began to decline in the late 1950s (see Figure 7). The Northeast was locked out of the tremendous growth in domestic sugar consumption in the postwar period. Brazilian sugar consumption increased by 16 million bags between 1945 and 1955; São Paulo increased production by 9 million bags during that period to capture over 56 percent of the increase in the domestic market.

In spite of the subsidy the northeastern producers received for selling their sugar on the international market (which made up the difference be-

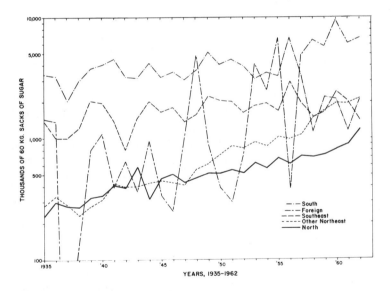

FIGURE 7. Regional and foreign sugar exports from major northeastern states, 1935–62. NOTE: Semilogarithmic scale. Exports are from Paraíba, Pernambuco, Alagoas, Sergipe, and Bahia. "Other Northeast" includes Maranhão, Piauí, Ceará, and Rio Grande do Norte. For states included in other regions, see Figure 1. Exports to Central West were insignificant. (Data from *Anuário Açucareiro*, various years.)

tween the world market price and the higher domestic price), they were aware of the risks of depending on a market beyond their power to control. When Getulio Vargas appointed Gileno dé Carli, a Pernambuco politician, to head the IAA in 1951, Carli's first act was to equalize the prices paid by the IAA to the sugar producers of the various states (Carli, p. 7). Before 1951, São Paulo producers received a price equal to the northeastern price plus the cost of shipping from Recife to Santos. This practice stemmed from the price structure in existence before production controls were established early in the 1930s. Removal of the additional price incentive, however, failed to stop expansion of the São Paulo sugar industry. In 1954, Carli explained the situation in an offical letter to President Vargas:

> But, restricting the greater profits of the South has still not been sufficient to thwart its rate of expansion in the sugar production sector, particularly in the state of São Paulo. In the present crop year, 1953 / 54, the state of São Paulo, even after suffering a frost, will produce about eleven million sacks, surpassing Pernambuco by nearly two million sacks. With this rapid expansion, São Paulo practically dominates the entire Paulista market, is invading the states of Paraná and Santa Catarina, states that used to depend on Northeastern sugar; and, moreover, is reaching the state of Rio Grande do Sul. This unhoped-for competition is detrimental to the future of the Northeastern sugar industry, an industry that can no longer place its sugar in its greatest traditional markets. [Carli, p. 13; my translation]

Carli instituted other policies designed to save the Northeast's position in the domestic market. The IAA stopped financing equipment purchases by São Paulo producers; special loans were granted to São Paulo producers who converted part of their crop to alcohol; a new pricing system shifted the entire cost of export subsidies to producers who surpassed their quotas; and the Banco do Brasil was prohibited from making any loans in the sugar industry without the IAA's permission (Carli, pp 15–16). If these policies had any effects, they were short-lived. São Paulo sugar production dropped by a little over 1 million bags from 1954 to 1955, regained its 1954 level by 1956, then nearly doubled between 1956 and 1957 (see Figure 6).

Sugar production and purchases in the state of Paraná illuminate the failure of the Northeast to maintain its position in the southern market (see Figure 8). Until the early 1940s, the Northeast sold Paraná what amounted to the output of one medium-size usina. Paraná also purchased small quantities from São Paulo and produced practically no sugar itself. Paraná developed its own sugar industry in the early 1950s, while increasing pur-

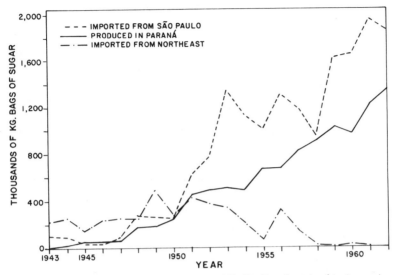

FIGURE 8. Paraná sugar production and imports, 1943–62. (Data from *Anuário Açucareiro*, various years.)

chases from São Paulo more than sixfold and maintaining, but not increasing, purchases from the Northeast. Through the mid-1950s, Paraná displaced northeastern sugar with its own production. The Northeast's last significant sugar shipment to Paraná was made in 1957. By 1961 Paraná was producing over 1 million sacks and purchasing about 2 million from São Paulo. The Northeast had been completely shut out of one of its traditional markets.

In 1960, when the United States terminated the Cuban sugar quota and reallocated it to other nations, it also increased purchases on the free (nonquota) market and prices rose accordingly. By 1962, the international price was higher than the domestic Brazilian price, and the export subsidy was changed to an export tax. This tax was earmarked for modernization of the northeastern sugar industry. Under these new conditions, the northeastern producers stopped guarding what remained of their position in the domestic market and began exporting their total surplus (Furtado, 1965, p. 138). Dropping their efforts to secure a niche in the Central-South market, they turned their political efforts toward the elimination of the export tax.

Northeastern efforts to eliminate the export tax were aided by the 1963 passage of the Rural Laborers' Statute—a law that extended minimum wage and organizational rights to rural workers. Furtado speculates that northeastern politicians allowed the statute to pass because they saw it as an excuse to press for the elimination of the export tax (1965, pp. 136–39). The political effort was successful: in December 1963, the IAA returned to regionally differentiated prices, but this time in favor of the Northeast. Northeastern producers received 6,478 cruzeiros for a sixty-kilogram sack of white centrifugal sugar—150 percent of the southern price (*Visão*, February 21, 1964, p. 26). In 1964, the Northeast was guaranteed the total of Brazil's U.S. sugar sales. In 1967 the domestic market was legally divided, and southern sugar was prohibited from entering the northeastern states (see Dantas).

The Northeast achieved its postwar sugar expansion without any significant technological improvements. While sugarcane output per unit of land improved moderately from the 1940s to the mid-1960s, it remained far below technical possibilities. Paraná's average yield was above sixty metric tons of cane per hectare, while Pernambuco was averaging less than forty (see Figure 9). Pernambuco's industrial yield (kilograms of sugar produced per metric ton of cane) actually *decreased* in the postwar period (see Figure 10). In the 1940s, Pernambuco's average industrial yield was over 100 kilograms of sugar per metric ton of cane; by the early 1960s it had fallen to 86.25. São Paulo was averaging 96.02 kilograms per ton. The

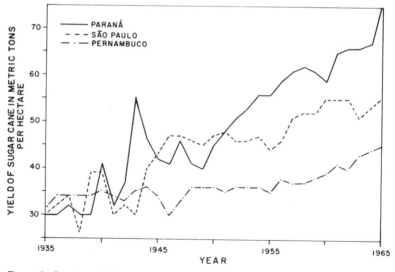

FIGURE 9. Sugarcane yields: Pernambuco, São Paulo, and Paraná, 1935–65. (Data from *Anuário Açucareiro*, various years.)

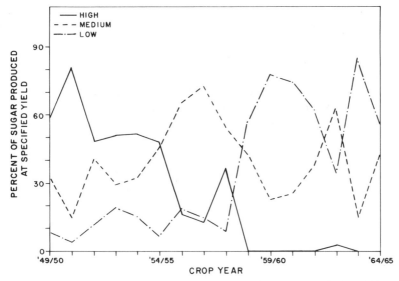

FIGURE 10. Industrial yield in Pernambuco, 1949–50 to 1964–65. NOTE: Yields of 101 or more kilograms of sugar per metric ton of cane are HIGH; 91 to 100 kilograms per ton are MEDIUM; and 90 or fewer kilograms per ton are LOW. (Data from *Anuário Açucareiro,* various years.)

Northeast's labor productivity was also lower than the South's: in Pernambuco, it took 3.6 man-days of labor to produce one ton of cane; São Paulo planters, with their higher level of mechanization, used only 1.2 man-days per ton (GERAN, p. 17).

Land productivity in the Northeast was increased primarily by the adoption of a high-yield cane variety, Co. 331 (3X). This variety accounted for about 80 percent of all cane in Pernambuco by the mid-1960s (Rosa e Silva, p. 81). Irrigation and the use of chemical fertilizers increased slightly, but both were still uncommon as late as 1967. The usineiros claimed that decreasing industrial yields were caused by the new cane variety, but Rosa e Silva believes that this variety has been a scapegoat for organizational and administrative problems. The Northeast's postwar increases in output were not accompanied by expansion of milling capacity. Rather than increase the grinding capacity of their mills, the northeastern mill owners extended the milling season—so a growing portion of the cane was milled either before or after its sucrose content had peaked. Pernambuco mills operated from 207 to 208 days per season, while the São Paulo crop was milled in 150 days. This extension of the milling season has been aggravated by "lost time," or time during the milling season in which the mill is not functioning. Lost time averages rose from 27.5 percent in the mid-1950s to 35 percent in the early 1960s. Poor coordination of field and factory operations was the major cause, and equipment breakdowns and labor disputes added to the problem. A study of one of the better-administered usinas in Pernambuco revealed that lack of cane deliveries accounted for over 50 percent of the lost time (Rosa e Silva, pp. 138–41).

By the late 1960s, the northeastern sugar industry was in a precarious position. It had lost its markets in the major consuming centers of Brazil. There was no guarantee that the special conditions that made the international market so lucrative would continue. Cuba was launching a major effort to increase sugar production, and any long-term success would certainly affect the free market sugar price. Additionally—and this is the subject of a later chapter—the Northeast's rapid expansion of sugar production set forces into motion that now threaten the region's entire political and socioeconomic structure.

8. Land Ownership and Labor Control: The Hypothesis of Class Collusion

One primary purpose of the ownership of large amounts of land, both on the individual and on the social level, is not to use it but to prevent its use by others.

Andre Gunder Frank

Increases in sugar production were attained by the northeastern states in the postwar era with virtually no technical improvements; the major factors of production—land and labor—were simply used in larger quantities. But the sugar producers could not increase at will the population or the amount of land in the zona da mata; so how were they able to draw increasing quantities of both into production? The answer lies in the transformation of the morador into a rural wage earner. The morador, working under the system of cambão, or condição, had, since abolition, worked several days a week for the engenho or usina in exchange for the use of a small plot of land on which he produced his own subsistence and an occasional marketable surplus. During the 1950s and early 1960s the plots were taken away. The sugar worker then had to obtain subsistence for himself and his family by working for a daily wage and purchasing his foodstuffs in the company store.

In a work written shortly before the 1964 coup, Celso Furtado analyzes this transformation of the rural labor system:

The extension of areas under cane cultivation had profoundly significant social and economic effects. The "morador," in a relatively short space of time, was transformed from a small sharecropper re-

87

sponsible for producing part of his family's food requirements, into a simple wage earner. From his confinement to an isolated hovel at the top of a hill, where his family had lived without any concept of neighborliness, he was pushed onto the edge of the road, no longer able to plant even "an inch of land" for food.

He would have needed a substantial increase in wages to buy himself the foodstuffs he formerly produced. In this way, the transformation from "morador" into mere wage earner brought about a rise in labor costs, with no corresponding increase in productivity. The "morador" was a semi-seasonal worker who went back to a partial form of non-monetary subsistence economy when there was a decreased demand for his labor; this made him an extremely cheap form of labor, since the land he used for his domestic crops had no alternative economic use. When a use was found for this land, the same worker needed a much higher wage in order to survive. Pressure for an increase in wages was accompanied by the pressure of rising real production costs, owing to the incorporation of inferior land. [1965, p. 132]

The reasons for the transformation of the morador into a wage earner, however, are different than those Furtado describes. He rarely accepts the orthodox position on anything without subjecting it to a severe examination, but in this instance he has. Neoclassical economic orthodoxy teaches that the entrepreneur purchases, leases, or otherwise brings resources under his control so that he can use them in their productive capacities; if the landowner reclaims land from the morador, then it must be to use the land. There is no question that vast expanses of new land were put into sugarcane production. Between 1953 and 1962, the land area in cane cultivation in the Northeast increased by more than 50 percent (GERAN, pp. 22–23). In 1963, a record harvest year, Pernambuco had 265,830 hectares in cane (CODEPE, p. 86). Yet, Pernambuco usinas *owned* 517,295 hectares (Rosa e Silva, p. 30). And usina-owned land only accounted for 49.1 percent of the cane harvest (see IAA). About 75 percent of the usinas' land was unused.

With so much unused land available even after Pernambuco sugarcane production surpassed 10 million metric tons, why would cane planters pay a cash wage when they had earlier been able to trade their excess land for labor? The answer is in the labor supply. High wages would have been necessary to attract enough new workers to the zona da mata to double sugarcane production. But the existing labor supply, the moradores, had been underutilized. Most moradores worked in the cane fields only one, two, or three days per week. By taking away the land the morador had formerly used, the usinas and engenhos were able to insure that he had no independent access to the means of subsistence. Thus the morador was forced to work six days a week in the cane fields for a wage set very near the minimum physiological subsistence level. It was the need for labor, not for land, that led the planters to reclaim the moradores' land. The land was taken not for use, but to withhold it from use.

According to the 1950 and 1960 censuses, the rural population of the zona da mata of Pernambuco barely increased in that ten-year period; yet the output of sugarcane, the major crop, more than doubled. Table 3 compares rural population growth with sugarcane production increases in the ten Pernambuco *municípios* that produce the most cane. In Table 4, these figures are transformed into the effective working population and the labor force needs of the cane plantations. The number of days of labor needed from *each* available worker doubled in a decade. These figures are verified by a 1964 study of rural workers which indicated that only 5.5 percent of the heads of rural families worked less than 201 days per year; of these, 65.6 percent gave sickness as their reason for not working more. The same study found that only 5.2 percent of the heads of rural families worked less than seven hours a day, and that 28.6 percent worked more than nine (Gonçalves, pp. 146–47).

Outside of Pernambuco and Alagoas, where sugar production did not increase as rapidly, the morador system of unpaid labor survived into the 1960s. As late as 1962, Usina Miriri in Paraíba, a 15,000-hectare plantation, was operating on the cambão system. Workers were trading one day of labor per week for the use of one-half hectare plots. Peasant League leaders showed the Miriri workers how they were being exploited: two years of work on this basis (104 workdays) were worth 12,480 cruzeiros at the prevailing agricultural wage, a sum equal to the value of the half-hectare plots. Workers' requests to pay a cash rent and abolish the cambão were met with threats of eviction, eventually leading to an armed battle between Miriri's hired gunmen and some workers. Two workers were shot to death and two usina gunmen were killed with *foiçes*, the crude sickles used to cut sugarcane (CIDA, p. 325).

An understanding of the political economy of the sugar regions of the Northeast requires the elucidation of several important concepts. The first is *withholding*—that is, the control of productive resources to prevent others from using them. The other is the effect of a *class* that exerts control over its members' economic activities. Class control restricts the means of pursuing profit that would otherwise be available to the individual. The in-

TABLE 3
RURAL POPULATION AND SUGARCANE PRODUCTION IN TEN PERNAMBUCO MUNICÍPIOS

Município	Rural Population		Sugarcane Production in Metric Tons		Population Ratio*	Production Ratio†
	1950	1960	1949–50	1960–61		
Catende	16,465	17,419	390,083	936,000	105.8	239.5
Riberão	12,701	13,325	253,155	580,480	104.9	229.3
Cabo	28,293	35,953	214,338	520,000	127.1	242.6
Agua Preta	29,961	28,390	419,842	425,000	94.8	101.2
Rio Formoso	16,863	18,732	132,927	508,170	111.1	382.3
Nazaré da Mata	33,137	33,503	141,034	297,600	101.1	211.0
Aliança	23,836	25,539	247,340	302,580	107.1	122.3
Sirinhaém	15,524	16,861	157,344	358,180	108.6	227.6
Escada	21,158	24,235	203,232	340,000	114.5	167.3
Timbaúba	25,415	28,077	107,724	298,000	110.5	276.6
Total	223,353	242,034	2,257,019	4,566,010	108.4	202.3

SOURCE: 1960–61 cane production data is from CODEPE. 1960 population is from *Anuário Estatístico*, 1962. 1950 population and 1949–50 cane production are from *Recenseamento Geral do Brasil* (1950 census).

NOTE: These ten municípios are Pernambuco's largest sugarcane producers.

*Population ratio is 1960 rural population as a percentage of 1950 population.
†Production ratio is 1960–61 cane production as a percentage of 1949–50 cane production.

dividual is restricted from profit-seeking activities that would threaten the economic position of the class. The individual may acquiesce to class directives because they are enforced by law, because he has been conditioned through an acculturation process, or because he realizes that to do so *is* actually in his own economic interest *in the long run*. The maximization of economic benefits then becomes a function of the class, rather than of the individual.

Class loyalties are just as important in developed countries as they are in underdeveloped ones; however, a developed country usually offers more opportunity for expansion and class control can remain highly flexible without becoming a threat to the dominant class. Where there are new markets to be captured, new products to be developed, and mass markets to be filled with cheaper versions of standard products, the individual capitalist can compete with his peers on many levels of economic activity without great risk of overnarrowing the political power base that guarantees the security of his property. In a stagnant economy, however, the stock of resources appears to be fixed, and the market often grows no faster than the population. In an underdeveloped society based on private property, maintaining control necessitates foregoing many forms of competition thought to be the hallmarks of capitalism in developed property-based societies.

For a small class of landowners to function effectively in an underdeveloped country, it must have institutions that make property ownership a determinant of economic power. John Commons's analysis of the role of

TABLE 4
WORKING POPULATION AND LABOR REQUIREMENTS FOR
TEN PERNAMBUCO MUNICÍPIOS, 1950–1960

	1950	1960
Sugarcane production, in metric tons	2,257,019	4,566,010
Labor requirements, in man-days	8,125,268	16,437,636
Rural population	223,072	242,034
Effective working population	58,072	62,929
Days of labor required per working person per year	140	261
Days of labor required per working person per week	2.7	5

SOURCE: 1960–61 cane production data are from CODEPE. 1960 population is from *Anuário Estatístico*, 1962. 1950 population and 1949–50 cane production data are from *Recenseamento Geral do Brasil* (1950 census).
NOTE: Labor requirements are based on estimated productivity of 3.6 man-days of labor per metric ton of sugarcane (GERAN, p. 17). Calculation of effective working population is based on figures given by Gonçalves. Average size of zona da mata peasant families was estimated by Gonçalves at 5.4. The family heads were responsible for 72 percent of family income. From this we can calculate 1.4 effective wage earners per family and approximately 26 wage-earner-equivalents in each 100 persons in the rural population.

these institutions in British and North American capitalism applies with equal force to northeastern Brazil:

> The transition from the notion of holding things for one's own use and enjoyment to the notion of economic power over others evidently accompanies the historical evolution of property from slavery, feudalism, colonialism and a sparse population, to marketing, business, and the pressure of population on limited resources. Where production was isolated, or the owner held under his control all of the material things as well as the laborers necessary to the support of himself and dependents, the concept of exclusive holding for self was a workable definition of property. But when markets expanded, when laborers were emancipated, when people began to live by bargain and sale, when population increased and all resources became private property, then the power to *withhold* from others emerged gradually from that of exclusive holding for self as an economic attribute of property. The one is implied in the other, but is not unfolded until new conditions draw it out.

This aspect of property becomes increasingly important as population pressure on natural resources occurs:

> Then the mere holding of property becomes a power to withhold, far beyond that which either the laborer has over his labor or the investor has over his savings, and beyond anything known when this power was being perfected by early common law or early business law. It becomes a power to extract things in exchange from other persons, in the absence of and wholly separate from individual human faculties—a power of property *per se*, silently operating but clearly seen and distinguishable from the manual, mental, and managerial abilities of its owner. [Commons, 1957, pp. 52–54]

The power to withhold is particularly potent when it is food (or the land that produces food) that is being withheld. Where land is abundant relative to population, the withholding of land from production can simulate the economic conditions of an overpopulated labor-surplus economy. That "ownership or control of land is power in the sense of real or potential ability to make another person do one's will" was verified by CIDA's mammoth study of land tenure institutions in Argentina, Brazil, Chile, Colombia, Ecuador, Guatemala, and Peru (Barraclough and Domike, pp. 397–98). Nor is the policy of withholding of food to guarantee a docile labor force unknown in industrialized nations. Investigators studying the food stamp program in the United States found that many employers claimed they were paying wages high enough to make their employees ineligible for food stamps when the wages were actually much lower: "We were told in two southern states that farm employers purposely make this implication in order to prevent families from getting commodities or food stamps on the theory that a hungry man will be a working man" (*St. Petersburg Times*, April 15, 1969). Several counties in Texas refused to distribute food stamps during seasons of high demand for agricultural labor (Estes, p. 14).

In sugar-producing regions, this aspect of land ownership is accentuated. After starting with slave labor, sugar planters in most of the Western Hemisphere became dependent on cheap labor. In addition—although this is becoming less true as fertilizers, irrigation, and new cane varieties allow a longer milling season—the sugar planters generally need workers for only a portion of the year and want a pool of unemployed to draw from during the peak of the harvest season. Boorstein, noting that the sugar industry of prerevolutionary Cuba used only about half of the total land that it controlled, describes the relationship of land ownership and labor control in the world's major sugar-exporting country: "The underutilization of labor-power and land in the countryside was enormous. But the idle labor could not get at the idle land because it was monopolized by the *latifundia*. The sugar companies had no interest in the full employment of the rural population. Their interest lay in unemployment. They needed a huge army of labor in reserve in the countryside for the cane-cutting season. One of the reasons they monopolized so much land was to keep the sugar workers from it. If the sugar workers had had access to land they would not have been available at miserable wages whenever the companies needed them" (p. 4).

Withholding land from production requires class rather than individual action. It would be difficult for one individual or family to monopolize such a geographically dispersed resource as land. When the *class* of landowners is attempting to limit access to land thereby to depress wages, any *individual* landowner will have the possibility of increasing production by hiring more labor. The class of landowners finds itself in a position similar to that of a labor union that cannot legally force its members to pay their dues; many individuals will attempt to receive the benefits of a class action without any of the sacrifices. For the northeastern sugar planters, the "dues" consist of the ownership of large amounts of unused land. Each planter is expected to eliminate a major portion of available land from production and thereby decrease the demand for labor. While increasing the concentration of land ownership would simplify class control, a smaller number of landowners would have more difficulty maintaining political power. Such a contradiction of goals can only be resolved by a compromise that provides the landowners with an adequate political base without dissipating the prerogatives of land ownership to the point that owning land ceases to be of tremendous economic benefit.

The foregoing does not imply any equality of ownership within the land-owning class itself. There is a great difference between those owning the largest amounts of land in the zona da mata of Pernambuco and those owning the minimum amount necessary to make them feel that continuation of the present land tenure system is in their interests. In 1964, there were 3,709 agricultural establishments of over 30 hectares each in the zona da mata of Pernambuco. These properties covered 1,194,348 hectares, or almost 88 percent of the total rural land in this region. Of these properties, 945 (covering 513,587 hectares), plus some additional smaller properties, belonged to the twenty-seven corporations that owned Pernambuco's forty-two usinas. An additional 35,414 hectares belonged to the individuals who were stockholders of the usina corporations (Rosa e Silva, pp. 20–24, 110). At that time, a maximum of twenty-seven families owned 40.46 percent of the agricultural land of the Pernambuco mata, and 45.97 percent of the land in properties larger than 30 hectares. The landholdings of the usinas themselves showed a great degree of inequality. In the early 1960s (when there were still forty-nine usinas in Pernambuco), two had fewer than 1,000 hectares each, six had 1,000 to 3,000, twenty-nine had 3,000 to

TABLE 5

NUMBER OF AND LAND AREA COVERED BY AGRICULTURAL PROPERTIES BY SIZE: ZONA DA MATA OF PERNAMBUCO, 1964

Size of Holding in Hectares*	Number	Percent of Total	Area	
			Hectares	Percent of Area
0–3	5,700	24.9	11,540	0.8
3–10	9,423	41.2	62,478	4.6
10–30	4,945	21.6	90,026	6.6
30–100	1,412	6.2	79,214	5.8
100–300	629	2.8	128,533	9.4
300–1,000	649	2.8	361,520	26.5
1,000–3,000	73	0.3	107,494	7.8
Over 3,000	1	0.0	4,000	0.3
Usina property	27	0.1	517,297	38.0

SOURCE: Calculated from data in Rosa e Silva, pp. 19–30.
*Land holdings categorized by size exclude usina property, which is all categorized as "Usina property," regardless of size.

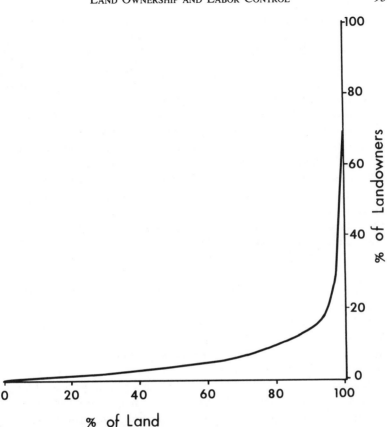

FIGURE 11. Distribution of land ownership, Pernambuco zona da mata. (Data from Table 5.)

12,000, seven had 12,000 to 21,000, four had 21,000 to 30,000, and one (Usina Catende) had 46,000 hectares (Rosa e Silva, p. 25).

Table 5 shows the percentages of land and agricultural properties in various size categories. In Figure 11, land distribution in the Pernambuco mata region is shown as a Lorenz curve. The Lorenz curve is a graphic description of land ownership inequality. Any point on the curve can be read on the vertical axis (which shows the percentage of agricultural establishments) and on the horizontal axis (which shows the percentage of the region's land area occupied by the corresponding percentage of agricultural establishments). A region with properties of equal sizes would have a perfectly straight Lorenz curve, cutting diagonally across the graph at an angle of forty-five degrees. A hypothetical region with 100 percent of the land

owned by one agricultural establishment and with a large number of agricultural establishments having no land at all would follow the horizontal
axis from 0 to 100 percent and then ascend along the vertical axis. The
Lorenz curve here is close to perfect inequality. In fact, this curve understates the region's land ownership considerably since the vast majority of
the rural population own *no* land and do not enter into the curve at all. The
rural population of this region was 830,856 in 1960 (*Anuário Estatístico*,
1961). On the basis of an average family size of 5.4 for rural families
(Gonçalves, p. 122), this would represent about 150,000 families. Less
than 15 percent of rural families, then, own any land. Additionally, except
for the usina properties, we cannot determine the extent of multiple ownership. Cross checks of census data with município records in several other
regions of Brazil indicate that the actual number of landowners is much
smaller than the number of agricultural properties (CIDA, pp. 101–6). All
farms in the Pernambuco mata of thirty or more hectares are owned by
2,791 families at most (Table 5). These properties cover 88 percent of the
region's total agricultural land.

Before looking at the methods used to limit production, we might ask
what choices would theoretically be open to a landowner who wished to
utilize his resources more fully—that is, what could he do to increase production or reduce the wasteful withholding of unused resources in the absence of controls and restraints? The landowner would have three basic
choices: to produce more sugarcane; to produce other crops for export, for
local markets, or for the Recife market; or to sell or rent his unused land.
As mentioned earlier, the extent of this unused land is considerable. The
usinas plant 1 hectare of each 4.5; the fornecedores plant 1 hectare of each
4.7 (Rosa e Silva, pp. 98–99).

On a superficial level, we can say that the landowner does not increase
sugar production because of quota restrictions. However, the quotas are established through the political action of the land and mill owners. This still
leaves us with the question of how the quotas benefit the sugar industry as a
whole and the planters and usineiros as individuals. Figure 12 is an abstract
diagram of the economics of the quota. In the 1930s, when quotas were established, the northeastern sugar producers were selling most of their sugar
within Brazil. Pernambuco was producing almost 40 percent of Brazil's
total sugar output. With a limited domestic market, the amount of sugar
produced affected the price at which it could be sold. At a lower price the
individual consumed more sugar in general and more usina (centrifugal)
sugar in particular. That is, the consumer increased his total consumption
as the price of centrifugal sugar declined, *and* he increased the proportion

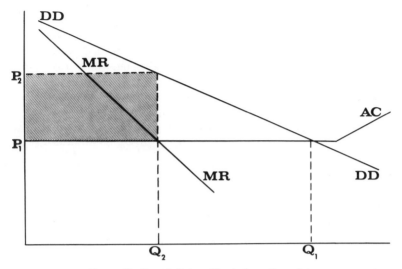

FIGURE 12. Sugar industry selling in domestic market.

of usina sugar in his total sugar consumption. This was a rather different situation than exists in industrialized countries (and in Brazil's Central-South) today. Where per capita sugar consumption has reached its maximum, sugar becomes rather price-inelastic—that is, consumers maintain their level of consumption whatever the price.

The response of Brazilian consumers to the price of sugar is indicated by the downward sloping domestic demand curve, DD (Figure 12). This simply says that sugar consumption goes up as the price drops; or, conversely, to sell a larger quantity of sugar, producers will be forced to accept a lower price. As the demand of the sugar mills for cane is derived from consumer demand for sugar, line DD also represents the demand for cane. Line AC is the average cost of producing a given quantity of cane. It begins by running parallel to the horizontal axis, indicating that, up to the point at which AC bends upward, increasing quantities of cane can be produced at constant costs per unit. With vast reserves of land at their disposal and with relative underemployment of labor under the morador system, this is a fair representation of the situation facing the sugar industry of the Northeast until the early 1950s.

Following the neoclassical convention, "cost" includes a return to capital—that is, a "normal" return. A higher return (if new enterprises could enter at will and existing enterprises had access to additional capital) would cause capital invested in enterprises earning the normal rate to shift to the sector offering higher profits. A lower-than-normal return would cause capital to leave the sugar sector until the profit rate had again been equalized with the prevailing rate. Within the framework of assumptions on which neoclassical theory is based, production will increase until larger-than-average profits are no longer obtained. On the graph, this is the point at which the domestic demand curve, DD, intersects the average cost curve, AC. At that production level, the quantity Q_1 of sugarcane is being produced and this quantity will be sold in the domestic market at the per unit price of P_1. Gross revenue to the planters is P_1 times Q_i. As profits are normal, there is no incentive for existing planters to produce more cane and no incentive for outsiders to invest money in sugar plantations.

Of course, this analysis abstracts from many important aspects of economic reality. Sugarcane is subject to weather-induced fluctuations in output that are beyond the control of the planters. Entry of new producers is practically impossible in view of the land monopoly. And the power of the usinas vis-à-vis the planters prevents domestic demand for sugar from being smoothly transferred into demand for sugarcane. Yet, expansion of output under competitive conditions is, roughly, what happened in the 1920s. The weakness of the neoclassical competitive model, however, lies in the fact that any group with the political power and organizational ability to avoid competition will do so, and that is what happened in the 1930s. Rapidly increasing output of sugar depressed the domestic price at the same time that increasing world output was depressing the international price. Brazil responded to the crisis by abandoning its laissez-faire policy and giving the state the power to regulate key economic sectors. The Vargas government claimed it could establish a balance among four interest groups: mill owners, planters, sugar workers, and consumers. However, as often happens in such regulation schemes, those who can best press their claims—in this case, the mill owners first and the planters second—are able to insure that the regulating is in their favor. The yearly quota announcements still carry the same title as the pre-IAA regulation schemes: "Plan for the Defense of the Crop." The consumers and the workers have been forgotten.

Limitation of output, with legal or economic sanctions against entry of new producers, opens new economic horizons to the planters. Once the planters have found a way to distribute the quotas among themselves, the entire group can behave like a single monopolistic producer. Below the curve DD (Figure 12) is a marginal revenue curve, MR. Marginal revenue is the addition to total revenue obtained by a one-unit increase in production. The marginal revenue curve is more steeply sloped than the demand and price curve, DD, because to sell the additional unit of production, the prices of *all* units must be decreased. There is also a marginal cost line, but where each additional unit can be produced at the same cost as the previous unit, it corresponds to the average cost curve, AC. The producer—or, in this case, group of producers—who can limit output will restrict production to the point at which marginal revenue, MR, is equal to marginal cost. That is, the group as a whole will stop increasing production when the additional revenue to be gained from an incremental addition to production is equal to the additional cost of the incremental addition. Beyond this point, any expenditure on increasing production will add a quantity of revenue smaller than itself to the total revenue. This point is represented on the graph at the intersection of P_2, the price at which this quantity of production can be sold, and Q_2, the output level. Gross revenue, as in the competitive situation, is price times quantity. Cost, also as in the competitive model, is average cost times quantity. However, in the case of restricted production, total revenue is greater than total cost by the amount of the shaded area on the graph. And, as cost includes a normal profit, this shaded area represents a "superprofit" based solely on the monopoly position of the planters. Political compromise may prevent the planters from claiming the maximum possible superprofit, but any production level lower than Q_1 will be to the advantage of the planters.

Figure 13 depicts the response of an individual cane planter to competitive and monopolistic situations. An individual planter cannot produce

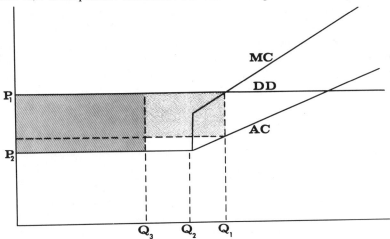

FIGURE 13. Sugar planter selling in domestic market.

enough sugar to affect the domestic price. The demand curve which he faces, DD, is a constant price, P_1. With land and managerial limitations, the planter's cost curve, AC, is constant in the lower levels of production, then rises sharply. The marginal cost curve, MC, corresponds to the average cost curve before it bends upward, then is more steeply sloped than AC. Here, too, cost includes normal profit. Under competitive conditions, the cane planter will increase production until the costs of producing an additional unit of output are equal to the return from the additional unit: that is, the point at which marginal cost, MC, is equal to price, P_1. If only one planter produces at this level, he can achieve the superprofits denoted by the dotted area (the difference between return and cost at output Q_1 and price P_1). However, there is nothing to prevent other planters from chasing this same high profit level. And, if they do, the price level will fall to P_2, the point at which revenue is equal to cost. The individual planter's production will fall to Q_2, and no one will make superprofits. But by agreeing to restrict production and by erecting barriers against the entry of outsiders who would find the superprofits an incentive, the planters can set quotas at production levels such that price P_1 can be maintained. The planter represented in Figure 13 might, for example, have a quota set at Q_3 and receive the superprofits denoted by the shaded area.

As the Northeast fell behind the South in sugar production, its producers began to lose their control over the market. There was no guarantee that southern producers, operating under a different cost structure, would agree with the Northeasterners on production restrictions. At the same time that it was losing its influence in the domestic market, the northeastern sugar industry was entering the international market, over which it had *no* control. The new market conditions arising from Cuba's elimination from the United States quota market and from the channeling of Cuban sugar into Soviet Bloc markets (where it replaced planned increases in beet sugar rather than free-market sugar from other tropical countries), led both to the reallocation of the U.S. quota and to higher free-market prices. Thus, the demand curve faced by the northeastern sugar producers was no longer the sloping domestic demand curve of Figure 12, but became the foreign demand curve, FD, in Figure 14. Within the range of northeastern production possibilities, the foreign demand was perfectly elastic. No amount of sugar that the Northeast could offer on the international market was sufficient to alter the international price (P_1 in Figure 14), so the northeastern sugar industry had to accept the price as given. Yet, as greater amounts of sugar could now be produced in the Northeast without depressing the price, cost—rather than price—became the limiting factor. Since the rural popu-

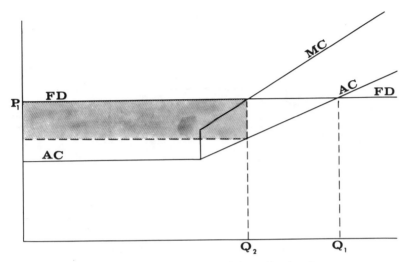

FIGURE 14. Sugar industry selling in international market.

lation of the zona da mata was not increasing, planters had to abandon the morador system and pay a cash wage. This is reflected in the graph by the upward turn taken by the average cost curve, AC. Production quotas and barriers to entry, which had previously served to maintain a high price, now served to limit the demand for labor. Under competitive conditions, the sugar industry would increase output until average cost, AC, equaled the international price, P_1. Output would be at Q_1 and there would be no superprofits. By restricting output, however, the industry could maintain production at Q_2, the point at which the price received, P_1, is equal to the cost of producing the last unit, MC. At this level, the industry would obtain the superprofits indicated by the shaded area: the difference between total revenue and total cost.

The unrestrained individual planter (Figure 15) faced with the international price level, P, would tend to increase his production until his marginal cost, MC_1, equaled the price. His output at this point would be Q_1, and his superprofits would be the dotted area. To attain such a level, however, would be to encroach on the same limited labor supply used by the other sugar planters. And they, like the planter in Figure 15, would also be attempting to increase production until the last ton was produced at a cost equal to the price received. In this case, the workers would benefit from high cane prices. Costs would rise for all planters until the superprofits had disappeared. The planter of Figure 15 would decrease his output to Q_2, the

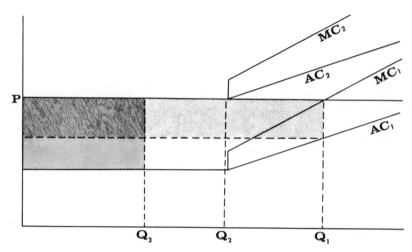

FIGURE 15. Sugar planter selling in international market.

point at which the higher average cost, AC_2 (at this point equal to marginal
cost), would be equal to the price. By restricting production, however, the
planter could regain a portion of his potential superprofits: if all planters
would agree to restrict production such that average costs remain at their
original level, AC_1, the planter would agree to accept a production limit
(Q_3, for example) that would not strain the labor supply. In this case, the
planter's superprofits would be the shaded area on Figure 15.

Sugar quotas are only the most formal—and the most visible—of the
many restraints on the economic behavior of large-scale landowners. The
other restraints are no less institutional than the quotas; and here we are
using John Commons's definition of institutional behavior as "Collective
Action in control of Individual Action" (1959, p. 69). The quotas only affect sugarcane: they in no way restrict the landowner from using excess
land for other crops. The widely encountered attitude that the zona da mata
is good for nothing but sugarcane is a myth. Manioc, the mainstay of the
peasant's diet, attains yields in the zona da mata that are double those of the
agreste and sertão. Pineapple, grown primarily in the agreste, attains its
highest yields in the zona da mata. Corn reaches higher yields in the zona
da mata than in the agreste, yet 41.18 percent of Pernambuco's corn is
grown in the agreste and only 3.37 percent in the zona da mata. Beans, cotton, tobacco, and coffee all attain relatively high yields in the mata region,
yet their cultivation there is virtually ignored (see CODEPE).

There are several direct economic reasons for the plantation owners' failure to diversify. First, shifting available labor from cane to other crops is only possible on plantations not owned or leased by the usinas; and where it is a possibility, the alternative crop would have to offer a higher return on money spent on wages. Also, shifting labor and other resources into a new activity is not as easy as some economists make it sound. The entire management system of the plantations is based on sugarcane and has acquired considerable inertia through four centuries of cane monoculture; it is not just a simple matter of relative costs. Theft is another factor. It is a common problem, cited by many peasants as a major reason for not raising small animals or vegetable crops. Sugarcane has a low value per unit of weight compared to other products. In 1963, a metric ton of cane was worth 3,100 cruzeiros, compared to 6,250 for manioc, 17,685 for sweet potatoes, and 27,159 for corn (see CODEPE).

But the major controls are institutional. To maintain his production of sugarcane and hire additional labor for other crops would neither violate the planter's quota nor jeopardize the secure income from sugar. The same is true of selling his excess land. That the planter neither utilizes his excess land nor sells it is a triumph of "Collective Action in control of Individual Action." Production of other crops would put pressure on the limited labor supply which, if extended throughout the region, would raise wages. Essentially, there is a tacit collusion among landowners to maintain a certain level of unemployment and thus keep wages at a subsistence level. Sometimes the interests of the landlords in maintaining a pool of unemployed in the region appear on the surface of political activity. In 1961, a group of northeastern senators tacked on an amendment to the bill providing funds for SUDENE that would have prohibited SUDENE from initiating colonization programs moving agricultural workers from one state to another. However, popular support for SUDENE became so evident—in the form of protests, petitions, strikes, and a student movement—that the amendment was eliminated (Hirschman, pp. 87–88). Still, SUDENE never executed its colonization plans on any significant scale.

Many neoclassical economists regard their criteria of economic efficiency as normative. When the laborer receives a wage equal to the value of the contribution to the productive process added by the last laborer hired (the marginal value product), he is receiving his due and efficiency is maintained. If the marginal value product of labor is above the wage rate, the farmer will benefit by hiring more laborers and by continuing to hire labor until—because of limited land or because he has to offer higher wages—the marginal value product and the wage rate are equalized. If all farmers function on this basis, each will finally be operating on a scale which equalizes marginal cost and average cost. There will be no superprofits and labor will not be "exploited" by being paid less than its marginal value product.

One study which measures the marginal value product of Brazilian agricultural labor is Youmans and Schuh's recent work on the productivity of agricultural labor in the southeastern state of Minas Gerais. Of the five municípios studied, three showed a statistically significant difference between the marginal value product of labor and the wage reported paid by farmers. In all three, the marginal value product was higher than the wage—triple the wage in two, and about seven times the wage in the other. The authors claim this situation must be due either to lack of knowledge by the landowners or their monopsony position with respect to laborers. They think it unlikely that the second condition holds, as "in each region there is a relatively large number of landowners, and it does not appear that they are colluding to keep wages down" (p. 951).

The absence of visible collusive mechanisms is no indication that collusion does not exist. In many parts of Latin America, collusion is institutionalized into the entire social framework of the land-owning class. This phenomenon is not limited to Latin America among regions or to landowners among bosses. A passage from *Wealth of Nations* is particularly instructive on this point: "We rarely hear, it has been said, of the combinations of masters, though frequently of those of workmen. But whoever imagines, upon this account, that masters rarely combine, is as ignorant of the world as of the subject. Masters are always and everywhere in a sort of tacit, but constant and uniform combination, not to raise the wages of labour above their actual rate. To violate this combination is everywhere a most unpopular action, and a sort of reproach to a master among his neighbors and equals. We seldom, indeed, hear of this combination, because it is the usual, and one may say, the natural state of things which nobody ever hears of" (A. Smith, p. 66).

Class control of individual economic activity through social sanction is a simpler matter than most economists suspect. Michigan State University's study of food marketing institutions in the Recife area indicates that commodity assemblers (who purchase foodstuffs from the farmers and wholesale them) are subject to a type of social sanction limiting the price they can offer the farmer. This is not a problem of dominance by several large buying firms, but occurs even though many small buyers make purchases in street markets and appear to be highly competitive. For example, there are 436 manioc flour purchasers in the thirteen zona da mata municípios nearest Recife. Of those surveyed, 65 percent agreed that "businessmen who pay more in order to buy more are not well regarded by others." Forty percent of the assemblers admitted that they had been asked by other assemblers to collude on pricing. The same type of social sanction operates among bean buyers. While only 32 percent of the bean buyers agreed with the above quoted statement, 70 percent of those who scored among the upper third on a "modernity index" agreed with it. The authors of the study believe that the difference (among bean buyers) might be explained by a lack of awareness of social sanctions on the part of the "traditional" buyers, as most have never attempted to increase their market shares. Those who scored high on the modernity index, however, are more "price-competitive" and have thereby come into conflict with social sanctions (Slater et al., pp. 9–14).

Occasionally, collective action by landowners fails. It is usually the outsider who causes the problems, a person not born into the land-owning class who does not properly understand the economic function of unused land. Antonio Callado, an editor of the *Jornal do Brasil*, reports on attempts by Pernambuco usineiros to stop a peer from leasing some of his plantations to his workers:

> This simple revolution [the Tiriri Cooperative, discussed in chapter 11] was made by an usineiro, Rui Cardoso, who is the son of a [textile] merchant who made a fortune. Rui doesn't have any old escutcheons to polish. He wants to produce and sell his merchandise and doesn't see why the sweat of the exploited peasant improves the taste of the sugar.
>
> It cost him quite a bit to lease his lands. The Association of Cane Planters of Pernambuco, trying to prevent this sacrilege, wanted to buy Rui's two usinas, which include 21 engenhos, for 1,700,000, 000 cruzeiros [$2,742,000], payable in six months. When the landowner refused, he was accused of Cubanizing Pernambuco. There was a newspaper in Rio that even said that the objective of Tiriri was to drive the 4th Army into a corner.
>
> And this wasn't all. The worst was the effort of the planters and mill owners, together with the Banco do Brasil and the private banks, to undermine Cardoso. They, the dubious nobility of the soil, wanted to spend all that money to prove that they were alive, that they couldn't be substituted with a cooperative, that they weren't an extinct race. Not succeeding, they tried to lock the coffers of finance to the new class of enlightened usineiro. [1965, p. 137; my translation]

Callado, however, is in error when he contrasts the traditional landowners, polishing their "old escutcheons," to the "enlightened" Cardoso. The landowners who attempted to buy out Rui Cardoso were not guarding a feudal past; on the contrary, they were protecting their own positions in a capitalistic future. They regarded Cardoso as an upstart who refused to pay his dues, a renegade who refused to withdraw an adequate amount of land from use and make his contribution to the maintenance of unemployment.

Those aspects of the Latin American latifundia often described as feudal and traditional—absentee ownership, vast expanses of unused land, the forsaking of food crops even when their price is high—really serve an economic function. That they serve this function on a class, rather than an individual, basis does not make them less economic, although present theory is inadequate for the analysis of this form of economic response. In the complex societies that cover most of the world today, a number of communities coexist in time and space, and many have distinct methods of conferring status or approval upon their members. Most have institutions that, in some ways, subjugate the individual to the society to preserve and continue the society itself. A subgroup that dominates other subgroups can only conceive of its own continuity in terms of continuing dominance. The continuing dominance of the usineiros and senhores de engenho of northeastern Brazil demands that, as a class, they maintain their superior economic and political position. We have noted that "tradition" has not prevented them from altering the labor system whenever it became economically advantageous. It is highly unlikely that an individualist economic ethic will sweep this class to self-destruction. Any effective challenge to the dominance of this land-owning class must be a challenge on a *class* basis. Such a challenge began in Pernambuco in the 1950s and is the subject of the next chapter.

9. Revolution in Pernambuco

We are never completely contemporaneous with our present. History advances in disguise; it appears on stage wearing the mask of the preceding scene, and we tend to lose the meaning of the play. Each time the curtain rises, continuity has to be re-established. The blame, of course, is not history's, but lies in our vision, encumbered with memory and images learned in the past. We see the past superimposed on the present, even when the present is a revolution.

Régis Debray

High international sugar prices led directly to the increasing impoverishment of the peasant who produced the sugarcane. He was forced to work more for less and was pushed below the previous culturally established minimum subsistence level. Since the land the peasant had received in return for his labor in the cane fields had been too small to fully utilize his labor, there had been significant leisure in his life. Now forced to work five or six days a week and prohibited from cultivating the land he had previously used, he was pushed ever closer to the minimum *physiological* subsistence level. Such a low standard of living had not existed in the Northeast since the crash of the world sugar market in the late seventeenth century had decreased the amount of labor needed by the plantations. The low point in the peasant's standard of living was reached between 1960 and 1962, when the northeastern sugar producers were expanding to capture Cuba's former markets, and before the effects of the new peasant political organizations had been felt. At that time, a day's labor was barely enough to purchase one kilogram of manioc flour (Furtado, 1965, p. 134).

This perverse reality of the Northeast—the inverse relationship of market dynamism to the living standard of the peasant—contradicts the conventional wisdom of orthodox economists. It has been common to describe Latin American as a "dual society," where a capitalistic industrial system is in conflict with a feudal and / or subsistence agricultural sector. One source of the confusion is the concept of subsistence agriculture. Clifton Wharton suggests that this confusion comes from using the single term "subsistence agriculture" for two separate concepts: the peasant's level of living and his degree of market orientation. We need two terms, "subsistence production" and "subsistence living," to describe the agricultural systems of underdeveloped countries (p. 47). The Pernambuco peasant who works for a miserable daily wage on a sugar plantation is engaged in subsistence living, but 100 percent of his labor is market-oriented. Before, when he worked on the terms of cambão, his living standard was higher, but he was engaged in subsistence production for that portion of his labor time that he spent on his own crops. If he could get more land—perhaps some of the unused land of the engenho—he could spend more labor time in subsistence production and thereby raise his living standard.

When the cane worker was displaced from his family plot, the zona da mata became more dependent on food from the agreste and sertão. Since cane workers and their families are 15 percent of Pernambuco's population, it is easy to picture the pressure on the food supply when the workers stopped producing their own subsistence and began to purchase their food. This added to the food shortage caused by sugar returning to its earlier inland margins of cultivation. Many engenhos on the fringes of the zona da mata had stopped cane production in the 1920s and 1930s when they could no longer compete with the usinas. The landlords rented land to their former workers. These peasants made the markets of Vitória de Santo Antão and other towns famous for their abundant fruits and vegetables. The postwar sugar market and cheaper truck transportation brought these areas into the orbit of the usinas, and the Northeast lost an important source of food (Andrade, pp. 109–10).

The sugar workers' standard of living was low by any measure. A 1961 survey indicated that adult plantation workers consumed 2,320 calories per day, about 75 percent of the recommended minimum. The same survey revealed that sugar workers spent 86.8 percent of their income on food (not including tobacco or alcoholic beverages); 0.1 percent of their homes had electricity; 0.4 percent had water filters (an important item where 60.4 percent of families got their water from uncovered wells and another 14.1 percent got theirs from rivers or artificial ponds); and no one surveyed had a gas stove (Gonçalves). Table 6 shows the weekly consumption of food by

TABLE 6
Food Consumption of Pernambuco Sugar Workers, 1961–1964

Item	Grams per Week per Adult-Equivalent		1964 Consumption as Percent of 1961 Consumption
	1961	1964	
Cereals	3,185	4,095	129
Bread	100	305	305
Rice	105	180	171
Beans	475	505	106
Manioc flour	2,315	2,890	125
Corn meal	390	215	55
Meat and fish	575	810	141
Fresh beef	135	205	152
Salted meat	350	525	150
Fish	90	80	89
Tubers	750	690	92
Sweet potatoes	245	135	55
White yams	280	125	45
Sweet cassava	225	430	191
Sugar	625	710	114

Source: Data from Gonçalves, p. 169.

adults living on Pernambuco sugar plantations. The dramatic increase in food consumption between 1961 and 1964 was a result of the increase in incomes after passage of the Rural Laborers' Statute and the negotiation of the cane workers' first collective bargaining contract, both occurring in 1963. These consumption increases are further evidence of the depressed living standards in the early 1960s.

The purchasing power of the sugar workers' already low wages was further reduced by the plantation stores. Although the practice is illegal, many workers are paid in *vales-de-barracão* (chits redeemable only at the small stores on the engenhos) rather than cash. The high prices, low quality, and dishonest weights at these stores are another means of exploiting the peasant. Food prices at the plantation stores are generally about 30 percent higher than in the towns (see Table 7). By selling food on credit, the company stores help to keep the workers in a constant state of debt, thereby tying them to the plantation and keeping them docile. Should the workers on any one plantation get far enough ahead of their obligations to make most of their purchases in town, the administrator often stops paying cash wages until the workers can take the case to court (at least two or three months). By the time the court orders the engenho to resume payment in cash, the workers are hopelessly indebted to the company store. These mechanisms were more common before passage of the Rural Laborers' Statute, but were still used during my stay in Pernambuco (1965–67).

TABLE 7
PRICES OF BASIC ITEMS IN COMPANY STORES AND PUBLIC MARKETS FOR
TWO PERNAMBUCO TOWNS, JULY 1965

| | Price per Unit in Cruzeiros | | | |
| | Jaboatão | | Vitória de Santa Antão | |
Item	Public Market	Usina Bulhões	Public Market	Engenho Bento Velho
Canned meat	550	700	500	750
Dried beans	550	650	400	500
Crackers	650	800	700	1,000
Coffee	140	160	280	100
Kerosene	135	200	200	200
Manioc flour	190	300	200	1,000
Matches	20	20	20	—
Rice	250	380	350	400
Salt	150	180	170	200
Soap	190	300	270	300
Sugar	250	300	270	300
Vinegar	80	110	—	—
Salted meat	1,600	1,700	1,700	—

SOURCE: Pearson, p. 18.

The revolution of peasant consciousness started at Engenho Galiléia, a Pernambuco sugar plantation. Cane had not been planted at Galiléia since the 1930s, when the mill was shut down. Galiléia was one of at least five engenhos owned by the Beltrão family in the município of Victória de Santo Antão. By 1955, 140 families rented land on the 500-hectare engenho. They paid a cash rent and produced manioc, vegetables, and bananas (Pearson, p. 101). It is not clear whether the Beltrãos were attempting to evict the tenants and return the engenho to cane cultivation, or whether they were taking advantage of increasing land values as sugar cultivation pushed its way back into Victória; but they did increase the land rent. In 1950 the land plots, averaging 3.5 hectares, were rented at about seven dollars per month. By 1955, rent had risen to twenty-two dollars (Callado, 1960, p. 34).

Because of the increasing difficulty of paying the rent, the Galiléia peasants organized a mutual benefit society to advance rent payments to members who had fallen behind and were in danger of eviction. The society was also formed to provide a decent burial. In a burial at public expense, the deceased was wrapped in butcher paper and carried to the graveyard in a municipal coffin, then dumped into the ground so the coffin could be used again. This offended the peasant, who desired to obtain in death a dignity he had never known in life (Castro, 1966, pp. 7–21). The society was formally initiated as the "Farming and Stock-Raising Society of the Planters of Pernambuco," and the landowner, Oscar de Arruda Beltrão, was asked to be its honorary president. Beltrão accepted. He thought the organization would simplify the one connection he, as an absentee landlord, had with the property: collecting the rent (Callado, 1960, pp. 34–35).

Beltrão's relatives and neighbors were more perceptive. They knew that *any* organization of peasants, however innocuous its initial goals, was dangerous. João Beltrão, Oscar's son, decided to get rid of almost everyone and raise cattle, and he ordered all members of the society off the property. But the Galiléia peasants had been relatively independent for twenty years; while they had paid rent, they had taken orders from no one. They were no longer typical of the peasant of the zona da mata, deferring to the senhor and sheepishly obeying his commands. They chose to fight the eviction order (Callado, 1960, p. 35).

Coming to their aid was Francisco Julião—a lawyer, an alternate state deputy in the Pernambuco assembly, and a member of the Brazilian Socialist Party (PSB). He took their case without pay. Unlike most educated Northeasterners, Julião could speak the peasant's idiom and could relate the legal and political aspects of agrarian reform to the peasant's limited world. He had earlier written a highly acclaimed book of short stories based on peasant life in the interior. Julião's part in the battle over Galiléia catapulted him into national prominence. Even the state's repressive actions rebounded in Julião's favor: "One day when he [Julião] was in Victória giving a talk in favor of the squatters of Galiléia, the governor of Pernambuco ordered the meeting to be dissolved by Captain Jesus Jardim. To this day the people of Victória laugh when they remember this violent Jesus who returned to Galiléia to capture and handcuff the deputy who defended the farmers. The scandal was a blessing. Julião became the first martyr of the Brazilian Socialist Party" (Callado, 1960, p. 37; my translation).

The litigation over Galiléia lasted four years. Julião presented a bill to the Pernambuco assembly that would disappropriate the engenho and give it to the peasants. The Brazilian constitution, however, prohibits disappropriation of private land, except on immediate payment in cash at the market value. And the Beltrãos were contending that the property was worth $100,000 (Callado, 1960, p. 142). Late in 1959 the situation became critical. In November, a group of Galiléia peasants who had come to town to parade in honor of the election of a mayor they favored were run out of town at bayonet-point by the Victória police. Later in November, a judge signed an order to remove the peasants from the engenho. Journalists predicted a bloodbath if police were sent to remove the peasants by force. In mid-December the crisis was resolved. The Pernambuco assembly passed the disappropriation bill and Governor Cid Sampaio, himself an usineiro, signed it (Callado, 1960, pp. 140–68).

While the Galiléia case was going through the courts and the assembly, the small society founded at Engenho Galiléia was transforming the peasants of the entire region. Its long and pompous name had been dropped for the simpler Ligas Camponesas ("Peasant Leagues"), a name originally applied by detractors. Under Julião's inspiration, Peasant Leagues were being formed all over Pernambuco and Paraíba, principally in the zona da mata and agreste. While it is impossible to determine the exact number of members, it is evident that the Peasant Leagues were politically important.

PLATE 1. Pernambuco peasants at a political rally, 1963. (Photograph by Peter Kurz.)

PLATE 2. Julião inaugurating Peasant League at Nova Olinda, Pernambuco, 1963. (Photograph by Peter Kurz.)

A 1963 estimate claims 40,000 members in Pernambuco alone. A 1962 estimate claims 80,000 active members organized into more than 100 leagues in the Northeast (Pearson, p. 119; Kurz, p. 52).

The effect of the Cuban Revolution on the peasant leaders of northeastern Brazil should not be underestimated. Just as the Latin American wars of independence and the constitutions that followed were influenced by the successful revolt of the North American colonists, the peasant-based land reform movements of Latin America today often take Cuba as their point of reference. Many northeastern peasant leaders visited Cuba, and they did not hesitate to report favorable impressions of a land without latifundia. In his study of the sociology of revolution in Brazil (before the 1964 coup), Irving Horowitz comments: "For the twenty-five million peasants of northern Brazil, the Cuban Revolution potentially represents the pragmatic extension of agrarian reform through political revolt. Geographical differences, climatic distinctions, population sizes, count for nothing when confronted with a singular hemispheric fact: Cuba has achieved agrarian rationalization, while Brazil has only rationalized about its agricultural dilemmas" (1964, p. 14). And Julião, in his speeches to the peasants, often referred to both Cuba and China:

PEASANT, I send you this communication. I have good news for you. Your cruel enemy, the latifundia, is not in good health. And I assure you that the disease is serious. It has no remedy. It will die foaming at the mouth, like a dog carrying rabies. Or like an old lion that has lost its claws. It will die as it did in China, a country very much like our Brazil. It will die as it was killed in Cuba, where the great Fidel Castro gave every peasant a shotgun and said: "Democracy is the government that arms the people." I was there and I saw everything, peasants. In Cuba there is no more *cambão*, nor *meia* [sharecropping on halves], nor *têrça* [sharecropping on thirds], nor *vale-de-barracão*, nor *capanga* [hired goons]. [Cited by Horowitz, 1964, p. 34]

Although illiteracy excluded the majority of peasants from voting, Julião and several other leftist politicians scored impressive electoral victories in the early 1960s. In 1962, Pernambuco sent Julião to the federal congress with more votes than any other candidate in the state (Kurz, p. 73). The other northeastern politician who rose to national prominence at this time was Miguel Arraes. Arraes was elected mayor of Recife in 1960 and governor of Pernambuco in 1962. Shortly before he was ousted in the coup of 1964, he was considered a serious contender for the presidency.

As Pernambuco's secretary of finance under Cid Sampaio, Miguel Arraes gained statewide recognition as a capable administrator. He had been careful to cultivate connections with leftists of all factions, and had the advantage of being known as a "man of the Left" without being tied to any particular party. When Arraes ran for mayor of Recife, in 1960, he was regarded as the only candidate who could unite the Left. He appealed to Recife's marginal population, a large portion of which was literate enough to vote. While other candidates talked about clearing the slums, Arraes promised to fill in swamps and create new slums:

In Recife many people don't even have a place to live. They have no place to put up a hut or a shack. I know workers who live in straw-roofed shacks precariously put up on the edge of the river. When the flood-tide comes, or when a storm hits, the "house" becomes an island. No one can leave or enter. To destroy *mocambos* [slum homes] as has already been done . . . without finding another place to live for the residents, is stupid and inhuman. . . . The mocambo is not a cause, it is an effect. It is a result of poverty and misery. It is better to have a mocambo than to have no place to live. It is better to have your own mocambo than to pay exorbitant rents for a rented mocambo—rent not just for the mocambo, but for the ground it is on. . . . To provide ground and housing, however crude and precarious, to the people of Recife who have neither—that is one of the plans of my government. [Cited by Barros, p. 53; my translation]

PLATE 3. Placard used in Julião's political campaign. Caption reads: "I am not thirsty for blood, I am hungry for justice. Justice is land, it is a home, it is bread, it is school, it is work, it is liberty, and it is peace."

As mayor, and later as governor, Arraes launched and expanded a unique program, the Popular Culture Movement (MCP). Its cornerstone was an extremely effective literacy program. With this phonetic system adults could learn to read in about forty hours—less than two months of classes. Instructors would start by showing slides and discussing them in such a way that students would understand the difference between the natural and the man-made world and would realize the unique potential of human beings. Then the lessons would proceed to the "generator words": sixteen words, all known to the illiterate, that contain all of the phonemes of the Portuguese language. These words also contributed to the politicization of the poor, as among them were *terra* ("land"), *povo* ("people"), *pobreza* ("poverty"), *classe* ("class"), and *eleição* ("election") (Callado, 1965, pp. 123–33). When Arraes was elected governor, this program was extended throughout the state with the help of radio programs. It is impossible to estimate how many learned to read through this program. Although it only made a small ripple in a tremendous pool of illiteracy, its impact cannot be measured in numbers alone: many who learned to read through the MCP have become leaders among the peasants. I attended a meeting of approximately thirty-five Pernambuco rural labor union officials in 1967, three years after the program—branded "communistic" by the military—had ended. Of those thirty-five, thirteen had learned to read through the radio programs of the MCP.

There was never any doubt that Arraes, in his campaign for governor, would carry Recife by a large margin. The problem was the interior, still influenced by the local bosses. Fortunately for Arraes, the electoral lists had been examined in 1958, and 200,000 "phantom" voters—over 30 percent of the number of living voters in the state—were removed (Barros, p. 43). Nor was the control of the voters what it had once been. Truck drivers, heroes to many backlands people, talked about the accomplishments of Miguel Arraes wherever they went. The Northeast's minstrels—the poets who write, publish, and sell their works by singing them in the marketplaces—spread popular poems about Arraes. The new Northeast asserted itself. Arraes lost the interior by only 27,000 votes, while he carried Recife by 40,000 and won the election.

The dramatic success of the Peasant Leagues and populist politics brought competition and reaction. Once Julião had demonstrated the potential of organized peasant groups, the cane fields became thick with organizers, agitators, infiltrators, and representatives of official and unofficial groups. The United States increased its intelligence activities in the area by beefing up the Recife Consulate–based CIA staff from one to three,

training the local police in riot-control techniques, and—most impor-
tantly—clandestinely subsidizing the "moderate" peasant organizations
(Page, pp. 128–30).

The moderate organizations were led by the Catholic Church. Many in
the church hierarchy thought Julião and others were exploiting the peasants
for their own political purposes. Others merely wanted to offer a moderate
alternative to dampen the peasants' revolutionary fervor. In 1961, twenty-
six padres met in Jaboatão, Pernambuco, to discuss possible lines of action. Some wanted to offer medical and dental services; others thought the
church should sponsor its own peasant leagues. The tactic finally agreed
upon was to train peasants in labor leadership and help them form unions
which, it was hoped, would be recognized as their bargaining agents in
dealings with the engenhos and usinas. Two young padres, Paulo Crespo of
Jaboatão and Antonio de Melo of Cabo, formed the Pernambuco Rural
Orientation Service (SORPE), which set up rural union organization teams
throughout the zona da mata (Pearson, p. 164).

SORPE had several advantages over the Peasant Leagues. A large and
powerful organization with staff, jeeps, and places to hold meetings was
important to its success. Additionally, the specific goals of the unions—
better working conditions and higher wages—were more definite than the
distant land-reform-oriented goals of the Peasant Leagues. The means were
also more specific; while Julião would talk about some future day when the
latifundia would be abolished, SORPE organizers talked precisely about
what could be done right now: the formation of unions and consumer
cooperatives.

The CIA quickly recognized the potential of SORPE to absorb the ener-
gies of peasant leaders and to direct their evolving consciousness along reformist, rather than revolutionary, lines. Using the Cooperative League of
the USA (CLUSA) for cover, the CIA dispatched an agent, Timothy Hogen, to Recife in late 1962. By late 1963, SORPE was receiving CIA
money channeled through conduit foundations to CLUSA, then to SORPE.
The SORPE / CLUSA ties were not broken until 1967, when CLUSA's
CIA backing was revealed in the U.S. press. CIA attempts to directly influence the rural union movement through the American Institute for Free
Labor Development (AIFLD, originated by the AFL-CIO) were ineffective
until after the 1964 coup, although AIFLD was well established in southern
Brazil (Page, pp. 128–30, 155, 232).

Despite legal obstacles to recognition of the SORPE-sponsored unions,
five multi-município unions were recognized by 1962 (Pearson, p.
165). Soon after SORPE's efforts started, most leftist forces recognized the

superiority of the unions as vehicles for peasant power, and they entered into the battle to form new unions or influence existing ones. Passage of the Rural Laborers' Statute on March 2, 1963, defined the union structure along syndicalist lines. The rural unions followed the structure established for industrial unions by Getulio Vargas in 1937, which was openly modeled after the unions of fascist Italy (Alexander, pp. 59–60). This structure gave the federal government considerable control over the unions.

With legal recognition, the peasants rapidly won significant wage increases. The contract finally agreed upon was a piecework contract, specifying the amount of work required for various tasks for one day's minimum wage. There was some difficulty in arriving at the specific task levels. During one meeting, José Ermirio de Morais, federal senator from Pernambuco and owner of two usinas, tried to set the level for cutting good cane at 250 *feixes* (bundles of twenty pieces of cane) per day; a union representative retorted, "If *you* manage to cut 250 feixes in one day of work, we will agree to this item." The level was set at 200 feixes (*Visão*, October 4, 1963, p. 9). In November 1963, 200,000 Pernambuco sugar workers went on strike for forty-eight hours and won an 80 percent wage increase (*Visão*, November 29, 1963, p. 15). As indicated in Table 6, there were considerable increases in consumption of most foodstuffs between 1961 and 1964. Early in 1964, a shortage of meat became evident in the Northeast; SUDENE reported that demand for meat in the zona da mata had increased fivefold since the new wages had become effective (*Visão*, March 20, 1964, p. 9).

Celso Furtado expressed concern that these wage victories would create a "premature rigidity" by putting the peasants in a position of relative privilege vis-à-vis the rest of the Northeast's rural population. Just as the railroads in Brazil had failed to modernize when they could still have cut wages and dismissed unneeded workers, the northeastern sugar industry had "missed the best opportunity for laying the foundations of a viable capitalist economy." The entrenchment of the sugar workers, Furtado believed, would make it difficult to cut costs, as such a process would inevitably involve cutting back the labor force. Of course, Furtado could not have foreseen the 1964 coup and the restoration of power to the landowners that led to erosion of the sugar workers' wages. Still, his comments on the wider aspects of this successful wage bargaining bear quoting at length:

> The most important group of Northeastern peasants has become a privileged sector in terms of the peasant class as a whole. With their wages on a par with those of urban workers, and equipped by their

advanced organization to carry out all the advantages of social legislation, the peasants of the sugar zone will, within a few years, have
been transformed into a genuine rural middle class. A legally established money wage, with the social advantages it offers, places them
well above the typical sharecropper, artisan, or even smallholder.
The social movements in which they may participate will always be
directed toward clearly defined objectives and closely bound up with
their own interests, all of them translatable into the legal language of
contracts. Taking into account the existence of a great surplus of
manpower throughout the rural areas, the worker protected by a collective contract is soon led to demarcate the limits of his own interests, aware that he forms part of a privileged minority. [1965, p.
140]

Furtado's point is of considerable importance in the debate between
those who would alter society with one blow and those who would alter it
through successive reforms. The danger of the reformist approach—should
the reforms work—is that the masses, bound before by common interest,
will divide into factions with antagonistic aims. Julião and his followers
took the "one blow" approach and continued to press for land reform. The
Catholic Church opted for a more equitable distribution of the social product without demanding changes in the structure of land ownership.

The struggle for control over the peasant movement in the Northeast reflected a larger power struggle on the national level. In 1963, the political
parties were preparing for the 1965 presidential elections. The constitution
prohibited Goulart from succeeding himself. Leonel Brizola, the governor
of Rio Grande do Sul, had the most radical public posture of any of Brazil's
major politicians, but he was constitutionally ineligible for the presidency
because he was Goulart's brother-in-law. This left Miguel Arraes as the
only politician on the Left with broad enough appeal to win. Arraes and his
supporters hoped to maintain constitutionality, but prospects were not
good. Everyone expected a coup. The Right expected a coup by Goulart, in
the style of Getulio Vargas, Goulart's political mentor. The Left expected a
coup by the military. In October 1963, Goulart asked congress to declare a
state of emergency—giving the president virtually dictatorial powers for
thirty days—but even his supporters on the Left balked and Goulart with-
drew the bill before it went to the floor. Goulart also attempted to arrest
Miguel Arraes, but failed due to poor planning and lack of cooperation by
some military personnel. Arraes expressed concern over a possible coup by
Goulart in a *Jornal do Brasil* column early in 1964 (Skidmore, pp. 253–
302, 413).

Brazil's syndicalist labor laws gave Goulart an advantage in the battle for control of the unions. Goulart's minister of labor had the final say in cases of union recognition. Conflicting claims about union leadership in Pernambuco were supposed to be resolved by the regional labor delegate, Enoch Saraiva. The recognition issue was critical, as the recognized slate of officials would receive the union dues as a direct payment made by the employer. Alliances formed by the various power contenders were fluid. Julião complained that the Catholic Church, Goulart, and the PCB were conspiring against the Peasant Leagues (Callado, 1965, pp. 57–61). In a long battle for control of municipal and union offices in Jaboatão, the Peasant Leagues, Saraiva, Arraes, and the PCB apparently were temporarily united against Padre Crespo and his supporters (Pearson, pp. 170–72). Jaboatão is a suburb of Recife and a large portion of its population consists of industrial workers. Several workers' marches on Recife originated there, and the town was nicknamed "Little Moscow." In September 1963 the Crespo group won the municipal elections, but in November Padre Crespo was forced to withdraw his slate of candidates for union offices, so there was no clear victory. Whether Arraes and Goulart ever actually worked together is not clear. An editorial in the *Jornal do Brasil* on March 3, 1964, criticized Goulart for conspiring against Arraes for control of the Pernambuco labor movement.

The political nature of the rural labor unions became apparent after the 1964 coup. In a political environment favorable to their development, the unions had thrived. Many demands had been met. Official statements of military officers after the coup gave assurances that the collective contract of the Arraes era would continue to be honored. Two days after the coup, officers of the Fourth Army (Pernambuco) decreed the rural unions would continue to operate normally (Pearson, p. 195). However, the peasants had not obtained sufficient power to effectively press their demands in the absence of the government's *active* participation on their behalf. Before the coup, landowners had operated in a climate of fear. They had expected that, in an ultimate showdown with the peasants, the police would either intervene on the side of the peasants or not intervene at all. After the coup, they knew that the army, in spite of its reformist noises, was above all interested in maintaining order. This meant that "disorderly" means of pressing demands, such as strikes, marches, land invasions, and mass rallies, were no longer available to the peasants. The "orderly" means were primarily court actions, and these were time-consuming and costly. Even when successful, they usually resolved only the case of one individual or, at most, of the peasants on one engenho.

The collective contract itself, once the landowners regained the courage to interpret it in their own favor, became a major source of problems. For example, there are three categories of cane with different norms for cutting. Good cane (*boa*) is defined as "thin cane on clear land," and the worker must cut 200 bundles for one day's minimum salary. For average cane (*média*), defined as thick cane *or* cane on weedy land, the daily quota is 150 bundles. Poor cane (*fraca*), defined as being dispersed or surrounded by heavy weeds, calls for a quota of only 100 bundles. Other task-quotas are defined according to the hilliness of the land or the hardness of the soil. In ground clearing, the quota for "easy" land is three times the quota for "difficult" land (Callado, 1965, reproduces the entire contract). The rural labor union in Jaboatão (the union that I worked with in 1966 and 1967) had four salaried officials and the part-time assistance of a lawyer hired by the Pernambuco Federation of Rural Unions. These officials and the lawyer spent most of their time resolving grievances over the interpretation of piecework provisions of the contract. This left little time for strengthening the organization of the union. Most workers could not make one day's quota in one day of work, and union officials believed this was not due to the quotas themselves, but to their interpretation by plantation administrators. In addition, the adminstrators often shortchanged the peasants on payday, a practice that union leaders believed had increased since the coup.

One result of the difficulty of enforcing the contract was a marked decline in the peasant's purchasing power. Merchants in zona da mata towns still have pleasant memories of the "Era of Arraes," when peasants came into town on market days and bought chickens, rubber boots, radios, and even bicycles. After the coup, many had difficulty even buying batteries for the radios they had purchased earlier. A 1966 study of the nutritional status of peasants in the zona da mata indicated that the caloric consumption of sugar workers and their families had declined significantly since 1963. The 1966 caloric intake appeared to be about 65 percent of the 1963 level, although data from the two periods are not strictly comparable (Jorgenson, p. 4). As one peasant expressed the dilemma, "A day's wage used to buy a whole kilo of *charque* ["salted meat"], now it only buys half a kilo."

Although the military dictatorship did not destroy all of the programs and organizations that were reaching the sugar workers, only the moderate programs were permitted to continue and many of these were severely gutted. With Celso Furtado exiled and other top-level SUDENE officials jailed, SUDENE became little more than an arm of USAID; and its status was formally changed from an independent organization to a division of the interior ministry. Paulo Freire was briefly arrested, the reading materials for the literacy program were confiscated, and a new program—sponsored by USAID—was put under the control of Presbyterian missionaries. SORPE was allowed to continue, but kept on a short leash. Padre Melo was trusted by the army and allowed to name new directors for most of the rural unions; Padre Crespo kept his office only through the intervention of USAID officials (Page, pp. 203–37).

SORPE's ties with CLUSA were strengthened by a written program agreement signed in December 1964 (Hogen, p. 11). By the end of 1966, fourteen "mixed" cooperatives were functioning in Pernambuco. These operate primarily as consumer cooperatives, but the "mixed" charter eventually enables them to assist the peasant in marketing produce. In the zona da mata, the peasant has nothing to market; however, SORPE technicians have hoped that the cooperatives can break the cycle of indebtedness to the company store that keeps the peasant in bondage. The agreste cooperatives have been more successful than those of the zona da mata, as they have been able to sell animal feed and small farm implements—items the landless sugar workers cannot use. While the cooperatives have not generally been able to supply consumer goods at prices below the marketplace prices, they have stressed the advantages of quality produce and honest weight. The cooperatives have always made a point of paying their taxes, whereas most small-town merchants, who can easily alter their books, pay practically nothing (Hogen, pp. 17–18). I was told that the Bom Jardim cooperative, in its second month of operation, paid more municipal taxes than all of the town's merchants. The mayor was so impressed with this potential source of income that he began to enforce the tax laws.

SORPE's rural union development program—assisted after the coup by AIFLD—concentrated on leadership training, essentially the same policy followed before the coup. The Catholic organization had always complained that Julião's Peasant Leagues were in the hands of university students from Recife, or "asphalt peasants," as the church leaders called them (Kurz, p. 80). There was some truth in these charges. However, Julião, unlike the church, did not start with a nationwide organization with a staff in every município; he had to depend on whatever resources he could muster. SORPE's success in finding and training peasants of potential leadership ability, limited to middle-level leadership, was nonetheless astounding. It was not easy for the peasant, used to a routine life and taking orders, to regard himself as capable of directing his own destiny. Timothy Hogen, the CIA agent working through CLUSA, described the change that had to take place in the peasant if his union were to succeed: "The rural union represented the first experience for the peasant in democratic practices. It was the first time outside of the Sunday Mass that he met as a group with other members of his class. It was the first time that he was allowed to freely discuss his problems. It was probably the first time that he realized he was not alone in his predicament. Through the union movement the peasants began to develop a sense of class unity. Participation in the union gave him the opportunity to speak in public, to run for office, to vote. The natural peasant leaders who rose to the surface were given experience in group direction, in office management, in dues collection, in record-keeping, in handling of funds'' (Hogen, p. 14).

AIFLD's major program in the Northeast was the construction of ''peasant service centers.'' Three were built in Pernambuco (two in the zona da mata) in 1965 and 1966. In 1970, two centers were built in the sugar regions of Alagoas and Sergipe (AIFLD, p. 34). The Pernambuco centers, although built with USAID funds, are administered by the Pernambuco Federation of Rural Workers. SORPE and the Instituto Cultural do Trabalho (ICT), an educational institute associated with the University of São Paulo and partially funded by the AFL-CIO, utilize the centers for labor leadership and union management courses. Skills, such as carpentry, sewing, horticulture, and first aid, are taught to peasants and their families. Peasants who take part in an educational program at one of the centers live there for the duration of the course; they receive their food and lodging and a small sum to support their families while they are not working. Cooperative training courses and literacy programs are also provided.

The noticeable North American presence in the Northeast brings up the question of indoctrination. In an address to graduates of one of AIFLD's labor leadership programs, George Meany denied that AIFLD's goal was to have Latin American labor leaders ''build a trade union movement in the image of the American trade union movement,'' then went on to warn against strong ties with a labor party and to stress that ''the chief function . . . of the trade union movement . . . is collective bargaining'' (Meany, pp. 11–12). The AFL-CIO's ''business unionism'' concepts could—if totally adopted by the peasant labor organizations—dampen the drive for land reform. The rural unions have already taken the public posture of not pressing for any benefits that might destroy the sugar industry. However, it is my belief that this is only a *public* posture, necessary if the unions are to survive. Private discussions with Pernambuco rural labor leaders have convinced me that land redistribution remains the ultimate goal of the rural labor movement. The president of one union said (in 1967) that he would press for the maximum benefits that the political system and the class cohesion of the union would allow: the goal is to destroy the sugar industry and get the land. The peasants are waiting for the right moment. One union official, commenting upon the Brazilian flag's motto, "Order and Progress," said that every peasant knows the motto means "progress for the rich and order for the rest of us."

10. Regional Disequilibrium and the Food Supply

If things were left to market forces unhampered by any policy interferences, industrial production, commerce, banking, insurance, shipping, and, indeed, almost all those economic activities which in a developing economy tend to give a bigger than average return—and, in addition, science, art, literature, education and higher culture generally—would cluster in certain localities and regions, leaving the rest of the country more or less in a backwater.

Gunnar Myrdal

Celso Furtado's 1959 report on the northeastern economy—the study commissioned by President Kubitschek in 1958—made four recommendations for the region's development. First, industrial investment was to be intensified. Second, and essential to accomplishment of the first, agriculture in the zona da mata was to be altered to insure an adequate food supply for the cities. Third, the agriculture of the sertão was to be transformed to resist droughts. And fourth, as the transformation of the sertão would make a portion of its population superfluous, agricultural colonies were to be established in uninhabited areas of Maranhão (CODENO, p. 6).

Part of the theoretical foundations of Furtado's development plan was the Singer-Prebisch theory of trade and underdevelopment. Prebisch described Latin America's economic relationship with developed nations as a metropolis-satellite framework (the metropolis, through its control over the terms of trade and other mechanisms, attains some of its development at the expense of the satellite). Furtado similarly described the economic relationship of the underdeveloped Northeast with the relatively developed Central-South. The basic concept of the Singer-Prebisch theory—that trade can be a cause of underdevelopment under certain conditions—has been

125

expanded by other theorists into a more complete theory of metropolis development and satellite underdevelopment. Myrdal has analyzed the "backwash effects" through which the market itself causes development to concentrate in one or several regions, thus sapping the development potential of other regions. While Myrdal postulates the existence of "spread effects" that reverse the tendency toward polarization when the developed region attains particularly high levels of industrialization, he notes that where regional disparities within nations have actually diminished, it has been because of government policies rather than unrestrained market forces (pp. 43–47). Frank discusses the metropolis-satellite relationship both of the United States to the Brazilian Central-South and of the Brazilian Central-South to the Brazilian Northeast (1967, pp. 143–218).

The development / underdevelopment theories are in complete opposition to orthodox growth and development theories. J. R. Hicks, an orthodox economist, notes that a region that develops first will tend to remain the center of further development, then observes: "There are regular forces which work against this concentration of wealth, so that they do something to even things out. There is at least some tendency for wealth to spill over from the centres, so that it induces some corresponding advance in the other parts. We can distinguish three ways in which this may happen, by *movement of goods*, by *movement of labour*, and by *movement of capital*" (p. 163, italics Hicks's).

Myrdal takes the opposite view: "Movements of labor, capital, goods and services do not by themselves counteract the natural tendency to regional inequality. By themselves, migration, capital movements, and trade are rather the media through which the cumulative process evolves— upward in the lucky regions and downward in the unlucky ones. In general, if they have positive results for the former, their effects on the latter are negative" (p. 27).

Hicks's statement that movement of goods tends to reduce regional concentration is based on the center's purchase of products from the periphery. However, the periphery also buys products from the center, and the balance of trade is usually in favor of the latter. Products manufactured in the center destroy many small manufacturing and craft operations in the satellite region. Stavenhagen notes this mechanism often "destroys the productive base for a significant part of the population, provoking what is known as rural proletarianization, rural exodus, and economic stagnation" (p. 19). Bottled soft drinks eliminate the vendors who blend and sell fruit punches, mass-produced plastic and metal dishware destroys the livelihood of local potters, ready-made clothes displace small-town seamstresses, and

Japanese-style thongs replace locally made sandals. Even the urban demand for food fails to benefit most rural people. If food is produced by many small-scale landholders, the terms of trade will generally shift in the favor of urban manufacturers whose monopolistic or oligopolistic positions enable them to limit output and control price. If, on the other hand, food is produced on the estates of a few large-scale landowners who are able to maintain favorable terms of trade, the peasant will not benefit even though the landowner will be able to purchase more products from the center.

In underdeveloped countries with policies designed to accelerate industrialization, additional forces operate to insure that trade favors the more industrialized region. First, these regions are affected by the widely discussed deteriorating terms of trade for primary products vis-à-vis manufactured goods. Second, national industries are generally protected by tariffs from goods produced in developed nations. The underdeveloped region cannot spend its foreign exchange earnings on finished manufactured goods from the countries that purchase its agricultural products. Manufactured goods must be purchased, at higher prices, from the national or foreign manufacturers operating in the more developed region. Thus, the underdeveloped region suffers the disadvantage of tariffs (higher prices for manufactured goods) without capturing any of the advantages (higher employment and industrial expansion). Additionally, both tariff and exchange rate policies generally favor importation of capital goods over consumer goods. As new investment continues to be concentrated in the more developed region, the underdeveloped region finds itself caught in a triangular trade in which it earns foreign exchange, that foreign exchange is used to provide capital goods for the national metropolis, and the national metropolis exports finished manufactured goods to the national satellite.

The exchange rate and importation policies instituted to develop Brazil's industrial base were disastrous for the Northeast. Foreign exports were often more than 10 percent of the Northeast's Gross Regional Product (GRP). In many years, the Northeast was able to use less than half of the foreign exchange it earned to import foreign products. Table 8 shows the magnitude of the transfer of the Northeast's foreign exchange earnings to other parts of Brazil. From 1948 through 1960, foreign exchange equivalent in value to 4.8 percent of the region's GRP was transferred out of the Northeast. The amount remaining was barely enough to meet ongoing needs, and very little could be used to purchase new capital goods. In 1957, for example, 70 percent (by weight) of the foreign goods entering Brazil through Recife were petroleum and petroleum derivatives and 10 percent was wheat flour (CAPES, p. 70). Thus, the Northeast became a

TABLE 8
Transfer of Foreign Exchange Earned by Northeastern Exports, 1948–1960

Year	Gross Regional Product (GRP)*	U.S. Dollars (in thousands)			Imports as % of Exports	Balance as % of GRP
		Exports	Imports	Balance		
1948	1,084.7	197.6	93.2	104.4	47.2	9.6
1949	1,253.9	133.0	100.3	32.7	75.4	2.6
1950	1,475.6	174.1	86.9	87.2	49.9	5.9
1951	1,786.3	197.6	166.4	31.2	84.2	1.7
1952	2,054.3	114.5	173.3	−58.8	151.4	−2.9
1953	2,176.0	169.6	95.3	74.3	56.2	3.4
1954	2,018.9	235.4	86.9	148.5	36.9	7.4
1955	1,934.6	238.5	86.2	152.3	36.1	7.9
1956	2,002.5	163.9	97.7	66.2	59.6	3.3
1957	2,187.3	212.1	131.9	80.2	62.2	3.7
1958	1,969.7	246.1	94.4	151.7	38.4	7.7
1959	1,774.3	216.1	79.3	136.8	36.7	7.7
1960	2,600.0	247.7	85.3	162.4	34.4	6.2
Total	24,318.0	2,546.2	1,377.1	1,169.1	54.1	4.8

SOURCE: Calculated from data in Baer, pp. 175, 272, 306, 169.

NOTE: Northeast here includes only Maranhão, Piauí, Ceará, Rio Grande do Norte, Paraíba, Pernambuco, and Alagoas.

*At official exchange rate. This rate sometimes fell to less than half of the free-market rate, so this figure overstates the GRP considerably.

market for Central-South industrial goods while earning much of the foreign exchange that made the Central-South's industrial expansion possible.

While the foreign exchange transfer shifted the *type* of goods that the Northeast could purchase with its foreign exchange earnings, there was also a shift in the terms of trade against the Northeast which reduced the *amount* it could purchase. CODENO's figures show the price index of Brazilian exports falling from 100 in 1948 to 73 by 1960. At the same time, wholesale prices of goods the Northeast purchased from the Central-South rose from 100 to 756, while the exchange rate rose to only 481. Thus, the terms on which the Northeast traded its production for Central-South products had fallen to 48 percent of the 1948 level by 1960 (Baer, p. 178). This is the same process that Singer and Prebisch have described as undermining the purchasing power of Latin America vis-à-vis the United States and Western Europe.

There are two major economic tendencies that cause such a deterioration in the terms of trade. First, industrialized nations or regions are able to retain the benefits of increased productivity through both the monopoly power of large industrial units and the collective bargaining power of the industrial unions. However, even the largest plantations are small compared with industrial enterprises, and they have less control over prices. And when commodity prices are temporarily high, the agricultural worker still has little power to raise his wages. So agricultural productivity increases generally benefit the consumer. Second, demand for tropical commodities is neither price- nor income-elastic. Small increases in production can lead to disastrous drops in price and decrease total revenue. Demand for industrial products, however, is both price- and income-elastic (cf. Singer and Prebisch).

The movement of labor is another force which tends to increase regional inequalities. Orthodox economists regard labor movements as tending to reduce inequalities. Hicks claims that, under some conditions, the movement of labor is probably "the most effective" of the "various equalizing forces that operate within a country." Although he adds that "we should be careful not to expect too much from it," his reasons for the qualification are that not enough labor movement takes place to completely equalize regional wages (pp. 164–65). Myrdal, on the other hand, notes what Hicks has ignored—the selectivity of labor migration: "As migration is always selective, at least with respect to the migrant's age, this movement by itself tends to favor the rapidly growing communities and disfavor the others. . . . the poorer regions will also have relatively higher fertility. This adds its influence to that of the net emigration in making the age distribution in these regions unfavorable; in the longer run it may also cause a less favorable relation between total working population and resources. The poverty in rural regions of Europe during the long period of net emigration to the industrial centers—and to America—has a main explanation in the unfavorable age distribution there, caused by migration and in part also by the higher fertility rates'' (p. 27).

The effect of migration on the age structure of the population of Brazil's regions has been considerable. Figure 16 presents 1960 census data for age structures in the Northeast and the South as percentages of the national age structure, represented by the horizontal line at the 100 percent level. The structural disparity is more apparent for men than for the total population. This disparity is particularly accentuated for people twenty-five to twenty-nine years old; the Northeast has only 88 percent of the national proportion, while the South has 107 percent. For men in this age group, the Northeast has less than 83 percent of the national proportion, while the South has 111 percent. The Northeast has relatively high percentages of people too young and too old to work. Further calculations from 1960 census data reveal that for every man fifteen to sixty years old in the Northeast, there are 3.2 Northeasterners in other age and sex categories; whereas for every southern man fifteen to sixty there are 2.6 others. When we include women between fifteen and sixty as part of the labor force, the disparity between the de-

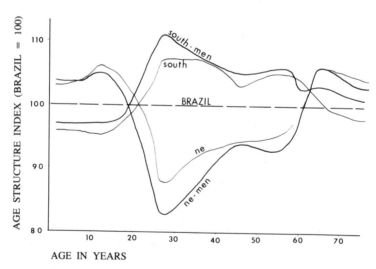

FIGURE 16. Age structure in Northeast and South. (Data from IBGE, 1960.)

pendency ratios of the Northeast and the South is lessened, but not significantly.

The Central-South gains extensive advantages from this migration. A study of migrants (not limited to migrants from the Northeast) in the cities of Rio de Janeiro, São Paulo, Belo Horizonte (Minas Gerais), Curitiba (Paraná), Londrina (Paraná), Juiz da Fora (Minas Gerais), Volta Redonda (Rio de Janeiro), and Americana (São Paulo) revealed that only 25.8 percent of the adults in those cities had been born there. Of the migrants, 66.5 percent had migrated between the ages of fifteen and thirty-nine, and 51.3 percent had migrated between the ages of fifteen and twenty-nine (B. Hutchinson, p. 43).

Capital flows are another factor which orthodox economists see as an equalizing force and which Myrdal and others see as another force adding to regional inequalities. Orthodox theory predicts that capital will flow to the region and / or sector where it earns the highest return. One factor which theoretically determines the return to capital is the quantity of labor and land available to combine with the capital. A region with abundant labor and land but little capital would be ripe for new investment, and capital would tend to flow to such a region until the returns there were the same as in other regions. A corollary of this theory would be that capital outflows from an underdeveloped region show the region lacks the capacity for investment.

Few development economists today, however, take the extreme orthodox position. The differences between social and private returns to capital are now commonly stressed (e.g., Belshaw). Many of the most productive potential investments in an underdeveloped region produce returns that cannot easily be captured by a private investor. Education and public health are certainly in this category. Other potentially productive investments are too large for private investors, and their potential returns are forthcoming only in the distant future. For example, building a major dam may take a decade, and extending a network of power lines that can deliver its entire output may take even longer. Without massive public investment in health, education, power, and transportation, private capital will continue to flow from the underdeveloping region to the developing region. The growth of modern banking and financial institutions will only accentuate this process. Myrdal notes that a banking system, in the absence of specific policies to prevent an outflow of capital from the poorest regions, "tends to become an instrument for siphoning off the savings from the poorer regions to the richer and more progressive ones where returns on capital are high and secure" (p. 28).

SUDENE planned to halt the growing regional disparities between the Northeast and the Central-South by industrializing the Northeast. Massive public investments in developmental infrastructure were planned. A tax write-off was designed to attract private capital. Brazilian corporations headquartered in the Central-South were exempted from up to 50 percent of their federal taxes if they invested twice the amount of the write-off in a SUDENE-approved plant in the Northeast. Other tax exemptions were established for new industries in the Northeast, including exemption from import duties on capital goods (Robock, pp. 159–60).

But the major element of the SUDENE industrialization plan was the SUDENE agricultural plan: Furtado and his staff believed that a cheap and dependable food supply was the primary key to industrialization. Underlying this concept was the recognition of a direct relationship between food prices and wages. Labor cannot be cheaper than the food and other subsistence items needed by the worker and his family. This principle was noted by the classical economists and summarized by Ricardo: ''The natural price of labour . . . depends on the price of the food, necessaries, and conveniences required for the support of the labourer and his family. With a rise in the price of food and necessaries, the natural price of labour will rise; with the fall in their price the natural price of labour will fall'' (p. 52). Similarly, W. Arthur Lewis notes that a large pool of rural workers living at subsistence levels is available for industrial employment at wages equal to subsistence plus urbanization costs (p. 410). Whether we accept Lewis's position that rural labor is underemployed and can be transferred to industry with no loss of food is not important here. Due to the monopsonistic position of the northeastern employers, the regional labor market behaves as if there were a labor surplus; and, under present conditions, many people are available to fill urban jobs at subsistence plus urbanization costs.

Minimum wage legislation does not substantially alter the subsistence-cost / wage-level relationship. Robock expresses concern that the minimum wage established for Recife (78 percent of the São Paulo minimum in October 1961) may inhibit growth of new industries (p. 148). However, the minimum wage is itself a political response to the workers' perceptions of the prices of subsistence goods. In the absence of a minimum wage affecting Recife's major industrial employers, the state would have to subsidize workers in some way or spend additional sums for police forces to control them. Lower food costs would permit a lower minimum wage as long as the relative political power of northeastern urban workers did not change. Additionally, it is not clear to what extent imposition of a minimum wage actually reduces employment. Joan Robinson argues that where employers have monopsonistic power, a minimum wage above the actual wage rate will increase employment as well as wages (1965, p. 295).

The SUDENE plan to reorganize agriculture in the zona da mata gave official recognition to what those who had to buy their food in Recife had known for some time: that market forces had not and would not guarantee that Recife and other mata cities would be fed at reasonable prices. Miguel Arraes made a green belt proposal part of his campaign for mayor of Recife in 1960 (Barros, pp. 56–67). To seize land in municípios surrounding Recife, however, was beyond his power, either as mayor or later as governor of Pernambuco. The Instituto Joaquim Nabuco de Pesquisas Sociais (IJNPS) made a similar recommendation in 1964, noting that the usinas in São Lourenço da Mata and Jaboatão could be moved to other states and that the lands they monopolized might be used for Recife's industrial expansion as well as for a green belt (IJNPS, 1964, pp. 44–45). Brazil is not the only sugar-producing country that has become concerned with the failure of market forces to provide food for its cities: Cuba began a Havana green belt in 1967 that was to encompass 30,000 hectares and increase the value of goods produced per hectare by *twenty times* (Huberman and Sweezy, pp. 125–27). The Havana plan, however, was well under way by early 1968, whereas no concrete moves have been made toward the establishment of a Recife green belt.

The northeastern cities' dependence on the interior for most foods has made the inland droughts a crisis for the entire region. For example, the 1958 drought cut Ceará's rice production by 82 percent, beans by 86 percent, and sweet potatoes by 76 percent (CODENO, p. 5). Even in good years, expensive transportation and numerous middlemen lead to a considerable divergence between the price paid the farmer and the price paid by the urban consumer. Miguel Arraes drew attention to some food prices in Recife that were 500 percent of the price paid to the farmers (Barros, pp. 56–57). The Furtado report claimed the agricultural producer in the Northeast was receiving prices 20 percent lower than his counterpart in the Central-South; yet the Recife resident had to pay (in 1957) 121.5 percent as much for a balanced diet as did the resident of São Paulo (CODENO, p. 62). Furtado and his staff were adamant about this issue:

> These data are of a most seriously alarming nature because they express a situation which, according to every indication, has a tendency to be aggravated. As land is a scarce factor—in fact for the most part monopolized by sugar cane cultivation—and as the population grows intensively, the Northeast turns increasingly to foodstuffs imported from the Center-South. Therefore, the trend of the price level

of foodstuffs runs upward in comparison to the Southern region, offsetting the small advantage derived from lower prices for foodstuffs of local production. It is a process that leads, necessarily, to the strangulation of the region's industries, which sooner or later will be unable to compete, within their own market, with manufactures from the South. We may state, therefore, that the weakest spot of Northeastern industries lies in the region's agriculture. [CODENO, p. 63]

Furtado's prediction that the food situation in the Northeast might deteriorate further was correct. Aracajú (Sergipe), with the lowest food price index of any northeastern state capital, has a higher food price index than Rio de Janeiro, the city with the highest food prices in the Central-South (see Table 9). The best Central-South city for the purpose of comparing northeastern food prices is probably Niteroí, a working-class suburb of Rio de Janeiro with food consumption characteristics similar to the northeastern cities. In Table 10, the yearly food price index numbers for several northeastern cities are shown as percentages of Niteroí's food price indexes. In the mid-1960s, relative foodstuff prices rose to levels reached previously only in drought years. These figures are even more astounding in view of

TABLE 9
Cost-of-Living Indexes for Foodstuffs in
State Capitals, January 1965

City	Food Price Index (1948 national average equals 100)
Northeastern capitals	
Recife	8,195
Natal	8,032
Maceió	8,030
Bahia	7,889
João Pessoa	7,801
Fortaleza	7,674
Aracajú	7,482
Simple average	7,872
Central-southern capitals	
Rio de Janeiro	7,053
São Paulo	6,672
Belo Horzonte	6,488
Vitória	6,466
Curitiba	6,442
Pôrto Alegre	5,885
Niteroí	5,840
Simple average	6,407

Source: *Boletim Estatístico*, pp. 33–38.

TABLE 10
RECIFE, MACEIÓ, AND ARACAJÚ COST-OF-LIVING INDEXES FOR FOODSTUFFS
AS PERCENT OF NITERÓI INDEX, 1948–1965

Year	Recife	Maceió	Aracajú
1948	114	99	92
1949	124	114	104
1950	123	108	114
1951*	131	120	110
1952	107	102	94
1953	111	98	95
1954	108	94	92
1955	107	87	94
1956	107	96	97
1957	122	101	96
1958*	133	113	108
1959	123	103	102
1960	124	110	105
1961	118	102	108
1962	121	120	123
1963	127	119	122
1964	135	129	125
1965	143	134	123

SOURCE: Calculated from *Boletim Estatístico*, various years.
NOTE: Index is cost-of-living-for-foodstuffs index for city indicated divided by cost-of-living-for-foodstuffs index for Niterói for same year, then multiplied by 100.
*Indicates drought year.

the fact that Brazil is one country and that transportation costs and the inertia of established trading channels are the only barriers to food movements.

Of the 1,359,154 hectares of agricultural land in the zona da mata of Pernambuco, only 243,564 were planted in sugarcane in 1963. Yet, only 75,648 hectares of the remaining land were planted in any of the other twenty-two crops which enter the agricultural statistics. The participation of sugarcane in the total agricultural activities of Paraíba, Pernambuco, and Alagoas is shown in Figure 17. Other important crops in the Pernambuco mata are manioc (25,770 hectares), coffee (12,056 hectares), corn (8,568 hectares), coconuts (7,480 hectares), cotton (5,798 hectares), bananas (5,513 hectares), and beans (4,683 hectares); see CODEPE. With the exception of bananas, the Pernambuco zona da mata is not self-sufficient in any important food crop. While self-sufficiency on a subregional level is neither necessary nor desirable on its own merits, the resources of the zona da mata indicate that many crops could be produced at a lower cost there than in the sertão or agreste. For example, large portions of the manioc consumed in the zona da mata are produced in the sertão; yet the average yield (from 1956 to 1960) in the leading sertão município, Araripina (over

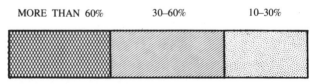

FIGURE 17. Percentage of agricultural income from sugarcane, by municípios: Paraíba, Pernambuco, and Alagoas, 1964. (Data from SUDENE, 1964.)

900 kilometers, mostly by unpaved road, from Recife), was only 7,186 kilograms per hectare, whereas the four mata municípios that produced significant quantities of manioc were attaining yields of 19,027 to 23,038 kilograms per hectare (CODEPE, p. 133).

Although the Northeast is primarily agricultural, it must import basic foods from the Central-South; 30 to 40 percent of the Northeast's expenditure on imports from other regions of Brazil is spent on food (Frank, 1967, p. 197). This restricts the region's capacity to increase its productive base through the importation of new agricultural and industrial capital goods. Many imported foods could easily be produced in the Northeast. A Michigan State University study of the Recife food market found that, in 1967, 23 percent of Recife wholesalers bought beans from the Central-South. Only 135 hectares of land in the Pernambuco mata were planted in rice, yet 26,417 tons of rice from the Central-South entered the Northeast through Recife in 1967. Pernambuco imported at least 22,000 tons of manioc from other northeastern states, as well as 3,000 tons from the Central-South in the same year (Slater et al., chap. 9).

Perhaps the case of milk is the best example of the distance between the potential and the actual in Pernambuco. Until the 1950s, most of Recife's milk was produced in Recife or its suburban area; then rapid urban and suburban growth displaced the dairy farms. The high value and rapid spoilage of milk would lead us to expect that the dairy industry, once displaced, would move into other zona da mata municípios and stay as close to Recife as possible. But the monopolization of land and labor by the sugar industry prevented such a movement. Most of Recife's fresh milk now comes from the agreste, primarily from São Caetano, São Bento do Una, and Pesqueira (which are, respectively, 150, 212, and 240 kilometers from Recife). And this supply is not adequate. At least half of Recife's milk comes from the Central-South as powdered milk. In 1967, the retail price of powdered milk was 40 percent above fresh milk. While many consumers undoubtedly prefer powdered milk, which is particularly convenient for people without refrigerators, Michigan State University's marketing study suggested that "the potential for pasteurized milk sales is indeed great in Recife" (Slater et al., chap. 9). And the potential for milk production is also great. Several studies indicate that the zona da mata has many advantageous conditions for livestock raising, including the possibility of using sugarcane waste products as animal feed. J. M. da Rosa e Silva recalled that as early as 1927 a well-known agronomist had advocated raising livestock in the zona da mata as a complementary activity to growing sugarcane. Rosa e Silva then lamented, "It is already 1965, that is 38 years later, and we have the same problems and are committing the same errors" (p. 125).

The Northeast is caught in one of Gunnar Myrdal's circles of cumulative causation. Without an adequate food supply, there is little hope for industrialization. Without industrialization, the Northeast's small surplus will continue to be skimmed off by the Central-South. Rapid industrialization would threaten the position of the landowners vis-à-vis the workers; but as long as the landowners monopolize the soil, there is little hope that industrialization will proceed rapidly enough to offer rural workers an alternative. The heavily subsidized industries entering the Northeast under SUDENE's guidance are hardly sufficient to transform its economy. At best, they will produce locally some of the items that have been imported from the Central-South. Like North American and Western European branch industries in São Paulo, the São Paulo branch industries in the Northeast will ship profits and royalties back to their home offices. The only real positive effect on the region will be the employment these industries provide, but manufacturing industries using some of the most modern productive techniques will have little employment impact on a region of 25 million people. The circle can only be broken on the agricultural side.

11. Some Attempts at Agrarian Reform

Unfortunately, some of our current discussion of land reform in the underdeveloped countries proceeds as though this reform were something that a government proclaims on any fine morning—that it gives land to the tenants as it might give pensions to old soldiers or as it might reform the administration of justice. In fact, a land reform is a revolutionary step; it passes power, property, and status from one group in the community to another. If the government of the country is dominated or strongly influenced by the landholding group—the one that is losing its prerogatives—no one should expect effective land legislation as an act of grace.

John Kenneth Galbraith

Padre Antonio de Melo, a founder of SORPE, believes the Tiriri Cooperative has given a death blow to the "three myths of the zona da mata": that nothing other than sugarcane will grow there, that cane can only be grown by a latifundium, and that the peasants are not capable of anything other than closely supervised cane agriculture. Visitors to the cooperative usually concur with the padre. "We used to have to walk three or four leagues to find enough firewood for the ovens in our houses," said one member, "but now we all have gas stoves." By 1967, just four years after its formation, the Tiriri Cooperative was an obvious success. Tiriri sugarcane was among the thickest to be seen in Pernambuco. Most members grew abundant supplies of manioc and beans, many marketed fruits and vegetables, and nearly all raised livestock. Many homes had outhouses and some families had wells with hand-operated pumps. In all aspects, Tiriri presented a striking contrast to the traditional engenhos.

Rui Cardoso, the usineiro described in chapter 8, responded to enactment of the Rural Laborers' Statute by leasing some land to the peasants.

Cardoso claimed that if he were to pay the minimum wage now required by law, he would have to dismiss about half of his workers. At one point, Cardoso asked SUDENE to take half of his field workers to Maranhão. SUDENE agreed, but the workers, elated over the passage of the Rural Laborers' Statute, refused to go. However, the peasants were interested in growing cane on a cooperative basis rather than as wage laborers. One cooperative had already been formed on lands that were formerly part of Engenho Tiriri. These lands, sold to the Great Western Railroad and abandoned except as a source of wood and charcoal, were "invaded" by thirty peasant families—supposedly under the leadership of the Peasant Leagues, in 1959. However, the lands were covered with leaf-cutting ants that destroyed everything planted; and, until SUDENE helped to form a cooperative and extended technical and financial aid, the peasants lived at a bare subsistence level (Callado, 1965, pp. 137–50).

An agreement was made among Cardoso, the peasants on five of his engenhos, and SUDENE. The land would be leased to the peasants. A contractual agreement would insure that sugarcane production would not fall below previous levels: 32,000 metric tons for the five plantations. Rent was set at 5 percent of the value (at prices set by the IAA) of the quota amount of sugarcane. Cardoso would purchase cane in excess of the quota amount, but the rent payment only covered the quota quantity. The rent compared favorably with rental agreements made by other usinas, which generally charged their fornecedores from 8 to 12 percent of the value of their cane (*Visão*, June 8, 1963, p. 40). The lease was for ten years, with the possibility of renewal specified. Land not needed for cane could be used according to the wishes of the peasants, except for reservations of subsoil rights and restrictions on the sale of forest products (Callado, 1965, pp. i–x).

Among the five engenhos was Maçangana, birthplace of Joaquim Nabuco, Pernambuco's famous abolitionist. The historical significance was not lost on the members of the new cooperative, who placed a bronze plaque on the casa grande of the former plantation: "On the *massapê* soils of the old Engenho Maçangana, where Joaquim Nabuco spent his childhood and received his inspiration for the campaign to free the slaves, we have accomplished today—one century later—the campaign to free the land, under the inspiration of President João Goulart, and through SUDENE and the Christian and democratic understanding of the rural laborers and of the owners of this engenho" (cited by Callado, 1965, p. 140; my translation). President João Goulart and Governor Miguel Arraes both participated in the contract-signing ceremony. *Visão* heralded Tiriri as a "new scene [*bossa nova*] in the zona da mata" (*Visão*, June 28, 1963, p. 40). Even *Brasil Açucareiro*, an official publication of the IAA, recognized the cooperative as an important experiment (*Brasil Açucareiro*, July–August 1963).

The cooperative covers about 5,000 hectares and contains close to 425 families. Each family can use more than 10 hectares. At the prevailing yields of about 40 tons of cane per hectare, the 32,000-ton quota can be met with only 800 hectares, still leaving more than 8 hectares per family

PLATE 4. João Goulart (left) and Miguel Arraes at the initiation of Tiriri Cooperative. (Photograph by Peter Kurz.)

free from sugarcane. Cane is grown as a cooperative operation, while livestock and other crops are predominantly family operations. Tiriri's proximity to Cabo, about forty kilometers from Recife by either railroad or paved highway, insures an adequate market for all the families can produce. Beans, manioc, citrus, vegetables, milk, and pigs are the primary products of the Tiriri farmers. Several peasants have expressed dislike of cane as a major crop; they only grow it because of the contract's terms and have not attempted to surpass the minimum quota.

Tiriri's significance is indisputable. Callado goes so far as to say, "one can only be opposed to Tiriri through bad information or bad faith" (Callado, 1965, p. 148; my translation). The same peasants who had worked the plantations before are still there. The only new resources have been technical aid and loans, and the peasants believe SUDENE has not met its promises on either. Yet more than 400 families that had previously purchased food in the street markets or at the company store are now producing their own food and sizable market surpluses as well. The gas stoves, water pumps, forage-chopping machines, small implements, housewares, and other items the peasants are buying indicate the potential market for industrial products. However, Tiriri does have some advantages that could not be transferred to a region-wide land reform of the same type. Less than 10 or 15 percent of the land in the zona da mata is so favorably situated as Tiriri with respect to the Recife market. Additionally, the high prices Tiriri farmers are receiving for their produce are a result of the continuation of the sugar latifundia elsewhere and would fall considerably if all land in the region were similarly liberated. Still, the land and the people have shown what they can do, given the chance.

The political barriers to the extension of the Tiriri experiment are still tremendous. As mentioned in chapter 8, the other usineiros regard Cardoso as someone who has refused to pay his dues and is profiting from their strength as land monopolists. Cardoso's main interest, the maintenance of a cane supply for his two mills, is protected by contract. He has not sold the land, and, given the peasants' attitude toward sugarcane, it is doubtful that he will. But even leases would not protect the mill owners if all or most of them were to lease their lands on the same basis. With several hundred thousand independent peasants as a new political force, the usineiros could lose the power to influence the price of cane, as this price is set by the IAA. Since the price of cane would be the usineiros' main economic link with the peasant, this price would be very important to both parties and would be the object of much political maneuvering. Moreover, with access to land, the peasant would no longer depend on the usineiro for subsistence—in John Commons's terminology, he would have more power to wait.

The most comprehensive government attempt to alter the land ownership pattern of the Northeast was the GERAN Plan. (GERAN is the Executive Group for the Rationalization of the Northeastern Sugar Agro-Industry.) GERAN was formed in 1965 as a coordinating agency composed of most of the official organizations operating in the Northeast. By mid-1966, GERAN had prepared a plan for the reorganization of the Pernambuco sugar industry—a plan which could only be described as cautious. One USAID technician observed that the proposal was inadequate as a solution to the economic and social problems of the zona da mata, but that it was, at least, implementable within the existing political structure and did contain some important elements of agrarian reform. The United States was prepared to give financial backing to the project.

The GERAN Plan was centered around the rehabilitation of the northeastern sugar industry. Field and factory operations were to be modernized to be competitive with the Central-South sugar industry. Land and labor freed by modernization were to be used in food production. Many displaced workers were expected to find employment in industry and commerce. The six- to fifteen-hectare family farms that were to be created would only absorb 25,000 of the 70,000 workers expected to be displaced (Jorgenson, p. 9). Each usina was expected to submit a plan stating the amount of land to be released and detailing the steps toward modernization. GERAN's deliberative council would have the power to grant or withhold loans—even the "between harvest" loans of the Banco do Brasil were to come under GERAN's control (GERAN, p. 51).

The land reform element of the GERAN Plan was the establishment of family cane farms alongside the cane lands retained by the usinas. The planners hoped to establish 14,528 family units of fifteen hectares each. It was expected that six hectares could be used for cane, two for "complementary crops" (manioc, bananas, fruit trees, corn, and beans), and three left in forest. One hectare would be for yard and buildings, and three would be unusable due to labor restrictions. These last three hectares would provide for income growth as possibilities of mechanization increased. Basing their calculations on a family with the equivalent of 2.2 full-time workers, and using current average zona da mata yields for all crops except cane, GERAN estimated that the family would initially have an income one-third greater than a family working on a salaried basis (the salaried family was assumed to be receiving the minimum wage and all established benefits and to be fully employed all year). Eventually, the planners predicted, the cane farm family would attain an income nearly double that of the hypothetical salaried family (GERAN, pp. 56–58).

Yet GERAN failed. As of mid-1970 the plan still had not been implemented and had gone through several revisions. Earlier, usineiros had attempted to water down the plan—to obtain its benefits in terms of new machinery for plant modernization while avoiding compliance with its agrarian reform provisions. New project norms were established allowing the usinas to keep a greater portion of their lands. Under the original plan, an usina with 23,000 hectares would probably have to give up 13,500 and diversify production on 4,500, leaving 5,000 for cane. Under the modified project norms, the same usina would only give up 3,500 hectares and would diversify production on 14,500 (Jorgenson, p. 10). Later still, the chairman of GERAN's deliberative council (also the president of the IAA) stated that the family farm proposals should be dispensed with altogether, that land not needed by the sugar industry should be divided into 150-hectare commercial units, and that basic food crops should not be grown in the zona da mata (Jorgenson, pp. 11–12).

Another modest government land-reform attempt, and one seemingly approved of by the military, was the Land Statute—popularly known as the "Two Hectare Law." Signed by President Castello Branco in 1965, it ostensibly guaranteed subsistence plots to all sugar plantation workers who had worked for one year or longer on the same plantation. The worker would have no permanent rights in the land: he would only be able to use it as long as he remained employed by the plantation; he could not plant fruit trees or anything with a vegetative cycle longer than one year; and the particular piece of land he could use might be changed from year to year by the landowner, effectively ruling out any improvements such as drainage or irrigation. The statute also specified that land used by the worker should be land not utilizable for sugarcane. The worker was not actually guaranteed two hectares; this was the *upper* limit of the land concession. Small families would have a right to only one-and-a-half or one hectare. The land could be up to three kilometers from the peasant's home. No plantation would be forced to concede more than 15 percent of its total land area. In spite of all the hedges against granting any real land rights, the Land Statute, although widely publicized, remained in legal limbo for nearly three years; implementation provisions were not approved until mid-1968 (*Brasil Açucareiro*, July 1968). Then, after waiting so long for a law the rural unions had had such great hope for, the peasants found it was to be implemented by the IAA, a condition that has rendered it basically useless.

12. The Strategy of Modernization

History records more frequent and more spectacular instances of the triumph of imbecile institutions over life and culture than of peoples who have by force of instinctive insight saved themselves alive out of a desperately precarious institutional situation.

Veblen

The root cause of the present state of uneasiness in Brazil is this simple truth: we know where the errors of our development lie, and we know that it is within our power to eradicate or minimize them.

Celso Furtado

Will the future of the Brazilian Northeast bear out Veblen's pessimism or Furtado's optimism? Probably neither. The time seems to have passed when an evolutionary revolution, guided by economists and planners, might have been the basis of modernizing reforms. Still, the "imbecile institutions" have lost the security they enjoyed for four centuries. Veblen, of course, could not have foreseen the coming of mass communications and the consequent awareness by people all over the world of the failings of the institutional systems under which they live. The poor in Recife's slums have seen foreign movies and occasionally watch television at a neighborhood bar or café, or through an appliance dealer's display window.

There are two widely differing views of the mechanism of change and of the form which the presently underdeveloped nations will eventually take. The Marxist vision is of old institutions being chopped away by a revolutionary group that has near-absolute power and does not need to compromise with the supporters of the old order. The opposing view—the

"Alliance for Progress vision"—is of a series of successive reforms; of popular forces exerting pressure through the ballot-box and gradually gaining a more secure position in the society; and of the gains of economic development eventually bringing all sectors of the population into the new society created by industrialization and agricultural modernization.

The Alliance for Progress vision has two distinct poles: economic and political. The economic goals are stated in terms of a rising per capita income. Growth will reduce tensions. The public investment that is so obviously needed will come from economic growth; neither the rich nor the poor will have to reduce their living standards to provide public and private capital formation, as long as per capita income rises. Politically, schools, urban living, and modern economic organizations are expected to improve the bargaining position of the poor. The poor, through education, will gain the political sophistication to elect leaders who will further extend public services and bring even more of the population into the modern sector. The national entrepreneurs, the growing middle class, and the organized urban and rural workers will realize their common interest and destroy the archaic and "feudal" agrarian structure.

The definition of economic development as a rising per capita income—central to the Alliance for Progress view—has been questioned by some economists. Furtado has redefined development as a change in the relative strength of the two poles of the economy: the industrial sector (including technologically advanced agriculture), which uses resources in rational proportions, and the backward sector, which is undercapitalized (1967, pp. 141–43). Per capita income, by itself, is not an adequate measure of development as "a given rate of capital formation might be sufficient for increasing per capita product and yet be insufficient for growth in the relative importance of the developed sector. Actually, if the developed sector increases its product without absorbing new contingents of labor, and if all population growth has to be absorbed by the backward sector at the level of productivity prevailing in that sector, then the rise in per capita income of the total population may not be accompanied by a relative increase in the developed sector. In other words, despite the rise in per capita income, the degree of underdevelopment is not altered comparably" (1967, p. 143).

The theoretical framework of the Alliance for Progress view has also been challenged. Economists who provided a theoretical justification for the U.S. foreign aid programs regarded underdevelopment as a transitory stage and expected the presently underdeveloped nations to go through a development process much like that of the United States and Western

Europe. They believed that a small boost in U.S. foreign aid to provide for capital accumulation could lift the entire underdeveloped world into self-sustaining growth (e.g., Rostow, p. 143). However, Furtado and others have stressed the unique process through which presently developed countries have passed. Capital accumulation in Europe and the United States brought more of the population into the industrial and capitalized agricultural sectors. These nations generally manufactured their own capital goods. They also had access to foreign markets for industrial products at important points in their histories. The presently underdeveloped nations are disadvantaged in both respects.

Once the populations of the presently developed nations were absorbed into the productive sectors, labor—its supply no longer elastic—was able to bargain for larger portions of the total social product. Increases in real wages then gave new impetus to development. "It is because an appreciable part of the new product is distributed among the working masses that development can continue" (Furtado, 1965, p. 48). However, wages are a major cost to the industrial enterprise; consequently, as wages increased, efforts to increase the productivity of labor through new technology were intensified. Pressure for higher wages (and shorter hours) was, then, one of the most dynamic elements of development. However, the major portion of the working population had to be absorbed by capitalized activities before such dynamism became operative.

How can today's underdeveloped nations absorb the masses into the capitalized sectors of their economies? Nations developing earlier created their own technologies as a response to cost conditions. Nations trying to develop today must accept a given technology that bears little relationship to available human and capital resources. Economies organized on capitalist principles depend primarily on market mechanisms to distribute income, but today's technology does not distribute income (through employment) to the same extent that nineteenth-century technology did. Soares's study of Brazilian industrialization is a case in point. Soares compared the percentages of Brazil's working population employed in the primary (agriculture and mining), secondary (manufacturing), and tertiary (services) sectors of the economy with other nations. He picked the comparative years on the basis of employment in the primary sector, as this is one of the best indices of economic development. Thus, he compared Brazil in 1940 with Finland in 1920, France in 1845, Italy in 1861, Sweden in 1890, and the United States in 1850: periods in which all of these nations had from 62 to 65 percent of their labor forces employed in primary activities (see Table 11). Similar comparisons were made for the Brazilian

TABLE 11
Sectoral Composition of Brazilian Labor Force Compared with
Other Nations and Time Periods: 1940, 1950, and 1960

| Country | Year | Percent of Labor Force in Sector | | |
		Primary	Secondary	Tertiary
Brazil	1940	64	12	24
Finland	1920	63	20	17
France	1845	62	18	20
Italy	1861	62	25	13
Sweden	1890	62	22	17
U.S.A.	1850	65	18	17
Brazil	1950	58	16	26
Finland	1930	57	23	20
Italy	1881	57	28	15
Norway	1890	55	22	23
U.S.A.	1860	60	20	20
Brazil	1960	52	15	33
Austria	1880	50	28	22
Canada	1881	51	30	19
Denmark	1880	52	24	24
Finland	1940	47	28	25
France	1866	52	29	20
Ireland	1841	51	34	15
Italy	1871	52	34	14
Sweden	1910	49	32	19
U.S.A.	1880	50	25	25

Source: Soares, pp. 192–94.

employment structure in 1950 and 1960. Soares found that Brazil had particularly high levels of tertiary employment and low levels of secondary
employment in all periods. Even after allowing for data from different nations and periods not being strictly comparable, the differences are so great
that the implication is clear: industrialization does not in this century create
employment to the extent that it did in the past. From 1950 to 1960, the
percentage of the Brazilian labor force employed in secondary activities actually fell; yet the most rapid industrialization of Brazil's history had occurred in this decade (Soares, p. 194). There is little hope, then, that industrialization will bring the Northeast's vast rural population into the modern
sector.

The political theories of the Alliance for Progress hold no more hope
than the economic theories. Many Latin American nations, Brazil included, prohibit illiterates from voting. Even when the masses can vote,
there is no guarantee that the candidates they elect will take office. The
commitment of Brazil's ruling classes to democratic government is not par-

ticularly strong, as the 1964 coup revealed. In the late 1950s and early 1960s, the masses in the Northeast picked candidates who would truly support their interests; the electoral victories of Francisco Julião and Miguel Arraes attest to this. With the disparities of income and wealth distribution in the Northeast—or in all of Brazil, for that matter—it is obvious that the politically sophisticated peasant or urban slum-dweller will attempt to elect candidates who will redistribute income or income-earning capacity (viz., land) in favor of the poor.

The founders of the Alliance for Progress put great hope in the growth of a Latin American middle class. A larger and more powerful middle class, they thought, would stabilize political and economic life. Not only has this not happened, but the middle class, attempting to preserve its own prerogatives, has often led the breaches of constitutionality. José Nun thinks that this phenomenon is of considerable importance in Latin American politics:

> In many cases, Latin American middle classes are threatened by the oligarchy or by the working classes, and *voting is one of the principal instruments of this threat.* Therefore, the army—that in the majority of countries represents the middle classes with all their contradictions—comes to the defense of the threatened sectors and *allows for political instability in defense of a premature process of democratization. . . .* there are enough reasons to see the Latin American middle classes as factors of political instability, whose instrument is the army, and whose detonator is precisely the democratic institutions that those sectors appear to support. This is a peculiar Latin American phenomenon that may be called the *middle class military coup.* [Nun, p. 147, italics Nun's]

Since reform seems unlikely, the next question is: what kind of revolution? The two Latin American revolutions that are often considered "models" for future revolutions are Mexico's and Cuba's. The United States now praises Mexico as an example for other Latin American nations to follow, after first disparaging it as "Bolshevik" and unsuccessfully intervening economically, diplomatically, and militarily (Frank, 1963, p. 72). Mexico paid a high price for political change: fourteen years (1910–24) of fighting and chaos, and an estimated 2 million deaths out of a population of 15 million—1 million directly from fighting and 1 million from famine and epidemics (Cumberland, pp. 241–72). Yet there were many accomplishments. The semifeudal agrarian structure was destroyed. Land was distributed to peasants under the communal *ejido* system. The power of the Catholic Church was broken. Landowners were forced to make their land productive or lose it. Most important, probably, of all the changes wrought by the revolution was the creation of a Mexican identity. The mestizo was praised as the ideal Mexican type. The peasant tilling communal lands became a hero of novels and murals.

Problems remain, however. A 1960s estimate of income distribution in Mexico indicates that 50 percent of the population receives only 15 percent of the total national income, while 1 percent claims 66 percent of the cash income (Frank, 1963, p. 74). As late as 1964, 29 percent of the population were still classified as illiterate (CED, p. 12). Many Mexicans are discouraged by the slow rate at which the benefits of an industrial society have spread to the masses: a 1957 study claims that only 35 percent of Mexico's population is benefiting from economic development (Casanova, p. 480). And this is in a country with one of the highest rates of growth of per capita gross national product in Latin America.

The changes unleashed by the Mexican Revolution undoubtedly created the preconditions for Mexico's rapid economic growth. The revolutionary government instituted policies that led to the growth of a new entrepreneurial class; increased the quality of human labor through education, public health, and the creation of an incentive structure stressing social and economic opportunities for the individual; increased the rate of capital formation in both the public and private sectors and directed capital into key sectors; and strengthened and expanded the scope of public administration (Maddox, 1960, pp. 266–78). The revolution also provided the political preconditions for growth—a system that was at the same time stable and flexible. Anderson and Cockcroft describe the Mexican political system as one which has been able to co-opt most important dissident groups— particularly those to the left of the government party (the PRI) who might otherwise use the government's own revolutionary rhetoric against it—into the single-party system through the concession of influence or the appearance of influence (pp. 376–82). Thus, the PRI has retained legitimacy in the eyes of most of the populace while avoiding violent outbursts of political activity that might jeopardize the economy.

Land reform was the core of the Mexican Revolution. Among Latin American nations, only Cuba has had a more extensive program. The most extensive land redistribution occurred between 1935 and 1940, when President Cárdenas distributed twice as much land as had been previously redistributed. One of his goals was to destroy the remnants of political power still held by the conservative land-owning class (Maddox, 1965, p. 385). However, the Mexican Revolution was essentially a popular movement; it was not made by the bourgeoisie. The initiative was generally taken by the peasants (O'Conner, p. 492). In Mexico, as in Cuba and Bolivia, the "disappearance of the latifundista oligarchy has been exclusively the result of popular movements, not of the bourgeoisie" (Stavenhagen, p. 23).

Mexico's agrarian reform could be most accurately described as a popular movement that modified capitalist property relations. While pre-revolutionary Mexico had many outward characteristics of feudalism, the large estates produced commodities for a market external to themselves— they were not completely self-contained. Ownership of the means of production (the land) by the upper classes assured their control of the surplus above consumption needs of their *peones*. Ownership of the means of subsistence (also the land) gave the latifundistas control over the labor force which assured production of the surplus. As the surplus was itself concentrated into a few hands, there was no dynamism on the market side and Mexico was locked into underdeveloped capitalism.

The land reform modified the terms of exploitation. By 1950, over 1.5 million families belonged to ejidos and over 1 million peasants owned their own small farms, giving nearly half the population direct access to the means of subsistence (Maddox, 1965, p. 387). Under these conditions, employers were forced to offer wages higher than the value of the minimum physiological subsistence. The *ejidatario* may still be exploited through credit or price mechanisms, but he does have independent access to the means of subsistence to a degree which he did not in the past. With the higher wages that must be offered under these conditions, the masses of rural and urban wage earners constitute a market that would have been much smaller without the agrarian reform. Returning to John Commons's terminology, the peasant now has greater power to wait: his bargaining position is thereby improved, and the income-spreading effects of employment become stronger.

There are, however, limits to the market dynamism obtainable through this type of land reform. Once a large portion of the population reaches a standard of living significantly higher than minimum physiological needs, access to a hilly, rocky ejido plot will have little continuing effect on the wage structure. To what extent the rapid growth of the Mexican economy has been due to market dynamism caused by the land reform and to what extent it has been due to other factors is not easily determinable; but agrarian reform does appear to have been a one-shot process, as far as its effects on the purchasing power of the masses are concerned. Without other non-market distributive measures, it is doubtful that the Mexican economy will be able to maintain its growth until all of the ejidatarios are absorbed into more heavily capitalized sectors. As long as the PRI retains some of the spirit of the revolution, we can expect that distributive measures in the form of minimum wage legislation and social welfare expenditures will continue. But the peasant still has received few of the benefits of development. The existence of such a large subsistence sector threatens the wage levels of urban and rural wage workers, who must depend on their influence within the PRI, rather than on any market power they might exert, to maintain or improve their levels of living.

Fidel Castro and his advisors faced different problems. Cuba's economy was closely articulated with the international capitalist system. Capitalist production relations, as well as capitalist property relations, pervaded the Cuban economy to a much greater depth than they had pervaded the pre-revolutionary Mexican economy. Cuba was a fully *underdeveloped* capitalist economy, whereas Mexico had many aspects of an *undeveloped* economy. While the Cuban agricultural worker lived in crushing poverty, he was not quite as poor as the prerevolutionary Mexican peasant. To guarantee the Cuban a subsistence plot of land would not have had the same radical effects that it had in Mexico. James O'Conner claims that Cuba's drift to socialism was the revolutionary government's response to problems that afforded no other solution, and that ''one can clearly make a case that socialist economic planning in Cuba was less an ideological product than an expression of hard economic necessity'' (p. 492). Mexico's revolutionary leadership was able to attain rapid growth while continuing to make important compromises with most of the powerful special-interest groups; but for Cuba, few prospects of economic growth were possible without the alteration of the power structure so that distributive, as well as productive, functions were centrally controlled.

While land reform was the Mexican Revolution's most spectacular element, the most striking elements of the Cuban Revolution were massive education and health programs. Illiteracy was reduced from 23.6 percent to 3.9 percent in one year; altogether, 707,212 adults were taught to read — and this was just the beginning of the adult education program. Magazines and other reading materials were specially prepared for new literates. We can contrast this with Brazil, where the lack of adult reading material accessible to new literates has seriously handicapped literacy programs ever since the Popular Culture Movement (MCP) of the Arraes era was outlawed. One of the abandoned MCP projects was the preparation of a special condensation of Euclides da Cunha's epic *Os Sertões* on the reading level of the new literates (*Visão*, June 21, 1963, p. 9).

Education on all levels has been given primary attention by Cuba's leaders. Cuban sources report that 27.6 percent of the island's population is enrolled in school, compared with 16.8 percent for Latin America as a whole and 15 percent in Brazil. Cuban higher education has been completely restructured with a new emphasis on science and technology. This successful educational program has been accomplished only because the revolutionary government chose to devote massive resources to education—and because it was able to tap the enthusiasm of thousands who moved from the cities to teach in rural areas. At $39 (U.S.) per capita and $141 per student, Cuba spends relatively more on education than any other Latin American nation—four times as much per student and six times as much per capita as the Latin American average (Huberman and Sweezy, pp. 22–52).

Cuba's educational accomplishments have been matched in the field of public health. Medical schools have been restructured with a new emphasis on hygiene and epidemiology (the latter was not taught in Cuban medical schools before the revolution). Every new doctor works in rural areas for two years after graduation. Cuba has the third highest proportion of hospital beds to population in Latin America, after Argentina and Uruguay. Gastroenteritis, polio, malaria, and typhoid—all major diseases before the revolution—have been virtually eliminated. By 1966, the infant mortality rate had been cut to 37.7 per 1,000 live births, the lowest in Latin America and only slightly above the rate for nonwhites in the United States. All this has been accomplished in spite of the fact that one-third of the doctors practicing in Cuba before the revolution fled the country (Huberman and Sweezy, pp. 53–64).

Any underdeveloped country that is seriously pursuing a development strategy will have to cope with what Helio Jaguaribe calls the "social crisis," a result of the contradictions between the inequitable distribution of income in underdeveloped countries and the masses' awareness of conditions attained by working classes in developed countries. This contradiction between expectation and reality creates a crisis difficult to resolve within a developmental framework:

> Neither the simple satisfaction nor the outright rebuff of such expectations is likely to be successful. If the expectations should be directly satisfied, either by elites prepared to compromise or by revolutionary counter-elites, the results would be self-defeating, since the inadequate accumulation of wealth and the low productivity of such societies would be aggravated by any real increase in the consumption ratio. On the other hand, if the marginal status of the masses should be maintained by force, and their expectations continue to be repressed, the end result would be no less self-defeating, since the

cause of the trouble—underdevelopment—would be perpetuated, and the political instability this generated would ultimately prove uncontrollable. [Jaguaribe, p. 44]

Mexico coped with its social crisis through the political co-optation process and the land reform; the latter created a subsistence sector which had not existed before the revolution. The ejidos, viewed from the aspect of mitigating the social crisis, are a labor reserve; they meet some of the immediate demands of the peasants and hold them until they can be absorbed by the more advanced sectors. This holding action may become less effective in the future, unless the rate of absorption can be increased. The impact of highways, bus transportation, radio, television, and newspapers on the rural areas is now in its earliest stages; it is difficult to envision the Mexican peasant remaining satisfied with his ejido plot and consequent low level of living for very long. Political co-optation is, to some degree, responsible for several groups in addition to the owners of capital and land— those groups best placed to apply political pressure on the PRI—being able to consume inordinate shares of the social product. The level of living of government and industrial technicians and of the best organized and most critically positioned labor groups is a barrier both to capital formation and to increasing the consumption of less powerful groups. The effect has been to maintain political stability without achieving the maximum potential growth of the Mexican economy.

Cuba took a different approach to the social crisis. From 1959 to 1961, it moved toward socialism in small steps. "Nearly every new measure," writes O'Conner, "drew some Cubans closer to the Revolutionary government and repelled others, leaving few indifferent" (p. 493). This process would not have been possible without the undivided support of the mass of the population. It was through the education and health programs that the Castro government obtained mass support without dissipating the scarce resources available for capital formation. Education and health programs *are* capital formation, and will probably bring a greater return, in the long run, than any other investment. Additionally, both programs could be implemented without drawing heavily on Cuba's scarcest resource, foreign exchange. From the point of view of the peasant or industrial worker, education and health are consumption goods. After food and shelter, they are the consumption goods to which the Latin American masses most aspire.

When change comes to Brazil, it will doubtlessly be rapid and thorough. In 1963, Celso Furtado could talk about the "duality within the Brazilian revolutionary process." Brazil's urban society could proceed gradually toward national development goals, while the agrarian sector would have to undergo rapid transformation. A Marxist-Leninist revolution, Furtado thought then, could only come about in Brazil if the agrarian structure were to remain immune to change within the existing political structure, or "as a result of social and political retrogression" (Furtado, 1964, p. 39). As Furtado—living in exile, his political rights suspended—certainly knows, the "open" aspects of Brazilian society which formerly negated both the need for and the possibility of a Marxist-Leninist revolution, no longer exist. The present Brazilian government, according to Jaguaribe, "is designed precisely to block the social changes needed for development of an endogenous and autonomous economy" (p. 191). As the contradictions between the existing form of government and Brazilian social and economic realities become greater, larger portions of the government's resources will be consumed by measures to maintain order. The longer such a government holds power, the less probable any gradual solutions become, for the buildup of fervent popular desires will prevent the military government from opening the slightest chink in its armor.

The Brazilian revolution will probably contain elements of both the Mexican and Cuban revolutions. A land reform in the Mexican style—with land use, but not ownership, passing either to individual peasants or to groups of peasants organized as cooperatives—will be a necessity of the first order for any revolutionary group wishing to establish legitimacy with the masses. However, the existence of radio and other mass media means that such a land reform will have to come by decree, rather than through slow administrative steps as it did in Mexico. Giving rights in land without granting land ownership will facilitate later and better-planned programs to capitalize agricultural operations. But the industrial aspects of the Mexican Revolution would be meaningless in the Brazilian context. State planning and state regulation of labor-management relations have existed in Brazil since the 1930s: the Brazilian petroleum industry is already nationalized, and the Brazilian government takes initiative in basic industries such as steel. In other words, many policies that have given a great impetus to Mexican economic development are already in practice in Brazil. This type of development ran its course by the end of the Kubitschek administration (1959); it was no longer possible to reduce the relative size of the underdeveloped sectors without antagonizing many powerful special-interest groups.

The brunt of any development effort in Brazil, particularly in the Northeast, will have to be in education and health. These public services have been neglected for so long, except in large cities, that the human capital which is a precondition for rapid economic development is nearly nonexistent. There are also, as in Cuba, sound political reasons for giving first priority to education and health. The poor in Brazil, and certainly the northeastern cane workers, will give solid backing to any government that stops promising schools and clinics and actually builds and staffs them. The literacy experiments of the Arraes era indicated the tremendous potential of Brazilian youth as volunteers in a popular education movement. But the neglect of basic education and public health is rooted in every aspect of Brazilian society, and the roots are more than four centuries deep, so the task will require years of unyielding effort.

What the role of sugar will be in a postrevolutionary Brazilian Northeast is impossible to predict without some knowledge of future world market conditions. The South can produce more than enough sugar for the domestic market on lands more suitable for mechanization. Probably very few of the sugar-producing units in the Northeast would survive the exigencies of central planning for social objectives. Both land and labor might be more profitably employed (from a social standpoint) in the production of foodstuffs and other commodities, as well as in industry, than in the production of sugar. Since many capital goods—roads and irrigation works, for example—can be built, if necessary, with little besides human labor, a centrally planned economy that is cognizant of the social and economic needs of the Brazilian people would have little trouble finding useful work for northeastern workers freed by the modernization or elimination of the sugar industry.

13. Land, Class, and Underdevelopment: An Overview

To put the matter rather bluntly, the plantation system must be destroyed if the people of plantation society are to secure economic, social, political, and psychological advancement.

George Beckford

The history of sugar in northeastern Brazil is the history of the dominant class manipulating social, political, and economic institutions so as to expropriate the maximum possible surplus from the rural workers. The major determinants in the evolution of land-labor relationships in that impoverished region have been the economic interests of the land-owning class, not feudal or traditional attitudes. The results of the concentration of so much economic and political power into so few hands have been a stagnant economy; an agricultural region that must import much of its food from Brazil's industrial regions; a society with extremely low health, education, and literacy standards; and, in the early 1960s, an open peasant rebellion.

Moreover, the northeastern sugar industry is moribund. It has been shut out of Brazil's domestic market by the more efficient sugar producers of São Paulo, and is dependent on internal subsidies and an external market of dubious viability. Brazilian policy makers of the late 1950s and early 1960s recognized that the sugar industry's domination of the best agricultural land of the Northeast inhibited the region's industrial advancement by restricting the potential food supply. However, all attempts to change the region's agrarian structure—no matter how mild, and whatever the concessions promised the land and mill owners—have failed. Even the innocuous GERAN Plan, which promised funds for modernization of the mills and

157

asked only that the landowners give up (with compensation) a small portion of their unused land, was shelved by the sugar interests.

The realities of the Brazilian Northeast defy traditional economic analysis. The failure, however, lies in our theory. Two points are important if we are to understand the reluctance of land and mill owners to "modernize." First, ownership of land serves an economic function even when the land is not used. While the concept of withholding resources for economic reasons is recognized by institutionalists, most neoclassical economists assume that the purpose of resource ownership is resource use. When slave labor was the backbone of the sugar industry, land ownership was not really important, as the labor force was itself owned by the plantation owner. When a growing population and a diminished international demand for sugar reduced the need for labor, slavery was gradually abolished. Although the labor force gained freedom in a legal sense, the ownership of land by a few wealthy and powerful families assured that the masses would have no independent access to the means of subsistence. They could be forced to work on the plantations for several days each week for nothing but the use of a small plot of land. After World War II, when new conditions in the international sugar market increased the amount of sugar that could be sold without disturbing prices, even the small land plots were taken away from the workers. In this way, they were forced to work five or six days each week for miserable wages.

Second, the control of labor through land ownership cannot operate on the basis of individual landowners. With land and labor generally underutilized, most landowners have untapped profit-making potential. However, if all landowners were to attempt to realize the potential productivity of their land and hire more laborers, the pressure on the labor supply would be too great to permit the maintenance of subsistence wages. So it is the *class* of landowners that is maximizing profits on a *class* basis. This requires that individual members of the class forego many attractive economic opportunities. Ownership of vast expanses of unused land might be compared to paying union dues: the individual is contributing to the maintenance of the economic position of the class. So the real strength of the land-owning class has been its ability to control its own members through both formal and informal mechanisms. Sugar production is limited by federal quotas. The number of landowners is kept at the minimum necessary to retain political power. The acculturation process within the land-owning families is also important. The only significant release of land by a northeastern sugar mill owner, the Tiriri Cooperative, was undertaken by an outsider who had purchased two mills. Most landowners are cognizant of the class nature of their power. They realize that schemes such as the GERAN Plan, while appearing to benefit them, will erode their power in time.

The plantation and mill owners have generally held the political reins in the northeastern states. They lost their control over free elections in the early 1960s when populist politicians responsive to the demands of the peasants and the urban poor were elected, but the coup of 1964 resolved the dilemma by abolishing elections and replacing elected officials (including elected union officers) with military-approved interventors. Development-oriented technicians who saw the land monopoly as a barrier to industrialization were also swept out of power.

Thus far, the only real threats to the positions of the landowners have been class movements by the peasants. Land seizures by the Peasant Leagues in the late 1950s initiated a series of political and economic actions by peasant groups. Rural unions were able to attain recognition as bargaining agents. From 1960 to 1964 the landowners were fearful and on the defensive. While the overt aspects of the peasant movement seem to be controlled by the military dictatorship, the gains won by the peasants during this period—though eroded—have not been forgotten. The northeastern peasant has become politicized. However, the low productivity of the regional sugar industry restricts the possibilities of alleviating social tensions through a more equitable distribution of the total social product without altering the structure of the productive base. A more rational use of land is certainly called for, and any land reform program must take into account the needs of the Northeast's urban population as well as those of the peasants. The present situation meets the needs of neither. Such reforms have little chance of success within the Northeast's—and Brazil's—present political and economic structure.

Bibliography

AIFLD. *American Institute for Free Labor Development, 1962–1972: A Decade of Worker to Worker Cooperation*. Washington: American Institute for Free Labor Development, n.d.

Alba, Victor. *Historia General del Campesinado*. Vol. 1, *Del Clan al Latifundio*. México: Centro de Estudios y Documentación Sociales, 1964.

Alexander, Robert J. *Labor Relations in Argentina, Brazil, and Chile*. New York: McGraw-Hill, 1962.

Anderson, Bo, and James D. Cockcroft. "Control and Coöptation in Mexican Politics." In *Latin American Radicalism*, edited by Irving Louis Horowitz, Josué de Castro, and John Gerassi. New York: Vintage, 1969.

Andrade, Manoel Correia de. *A Terra e o Homen no Nordeste*. São Paulo: Editôra Brasiliense, 1964.

Antoníl, André João. *Cultura e Opulência do Brasil*. Salvador (Bahia, Brazil): Livraria Progresso Editôra, 1950.

Anuário Açucareiro. Rio de Janeiro: Instituto do Açúcar e do Alcool, various years.

Anuário Estatístico. Rio de Janeiro: Conselho Nacional de Estatística, 1961 and 1962.

Arraes, Miguel. *Palavra de Arraes*. Rio de Janeiro: Editôra Civilização Brasileira, n.d.

Ayres, C. E. *The Theory of Economic Progress*. New York: Schocken Books, 1962.

Azevedo, Fernando de. *Brazilian Culture*. Translated by William Rex Crawford. New York: Macmillan, 1950.

———. *Canaviais e Engenhos na Vida Política do Brasil*. São Paulo: Edições Melhoramentos, 1958.

Baer, Werner. *Industrialization and Economic Development in Brazil*. Homewood, Ill.: Richard D. Irwin, 1965.

Baran, Paul A. *The Political Economy of Growth*. New York: Prometheus, 1960.

Barraclough, Solon L., and Arthur L. Domike. "Agrarian Structure in Seven Latin American Countries." *Land Economics*, November 1966.

Barros, Adirson de. *Ascensão e Queda de Miguel Arraes*. N.p., 1965.

Beckford, George L. *Persistent Poverty: Underdevelopment in Plantation Economies of the Third World*. New York: Oxford University Press, 1972.

Bello, José Maria. *A History of Modern Brazil, 1889–1964*. Translated by James L. Taylor and with a concluding chapter by Rollie E. Poppino. Stanford: Stanford University Press, 1966.

Belshaw, J. E. P. "Social and Economic Revolution for the Development of Backward Countries." In *Economic Development: Evolution or Revolution?*, edited by Laura Randall. Boston: D. C. Heath, 1964.

Boletim Estatístico. Rio de Janeiro: Conselho Nacional de Estatística, October–December 1965.

Boorstein, Edward. *The Economic Transformation of Cuba.* New York: Modern Reader Paperbacks, 1969.

Boxer, C. R. *The Golden Age of Brazil.* Berkeley: University of California Press, 1964.

Brasil Açucareiro. Rio de Janeiro: Instituto do Açúcar e do Alcool, various issues.

Callado, Antonio. *Os Industriais da Sêca e os "Galileus" de Pernambuco.* Rio de Janeiro: Editôra Civilização Brasileira, 1960.

————. *Tempo de Arraes: Padres e Comunistas na Revolução sem Violência.* Rio de Janeiro: José Alvaro, 1965.

Calógeras, João Pandiá. *Política Exterior do Império.* Rio de Janeiro: Instituto Histórico e Geográfico, 1927.

CAPES. *Estudos de Desenvolvimento Regional (Pernambuco).* Rio de Janeiro: Campanha Nacional de Aperfeiçoamento de Pessoal de Nível Superior, 1959.

Carli, Gileno dé. *A Questão Açucareira Nacional.* Rio de Janeiro: Instituto de Açúcar e do Alcool, 1954.

Carneiro, Edison. *O Quilombo dos Palmares.* São Paulo: Editôra Brasiliense Limitada, 1947.

Carneiro, Wilson. "A Concentração Econômica da Agroindústria Açucareira." *Brasil Açucareiro*, November 1968.

Casanova, Pablo González. "Mexico: The Dynamics of an Agrarian and 'Semicapitalist' Revolution." In *Latin America: Reform or Revolution?*, edited by James Petras and Maurice Zeitlin. Greenwich, Conn.: Fawcett, 1968.

Castro, Josué de. *Geografia da Fome: O Dilema Brasileiro, Pão o Aço.* São Paulo: Editôra Brasiliense, 1965.

————. *Death in the Northeast.* New York: Random House, 1966.

CED. *Economic Development of Latin America.* New York: Committee for Economic Development, 1966.

CIDA. *Land Tenure Conditions and Socio-Economic Development of the Agricultural Sector: Brazil.* Washington: Inter-American Committee for Agricultural Development (Pan American Union), 1966.

CODENO. *A Policy for the Economic Development of the Northeast.* Rio de Janeiro: Conselho de Desenvolvimento Econômico do Nordeste, 1959.

CODEPE. *Sinópse Numérica da Agricultura de Pernambuco.* Recife: Comissão de Desenvolvimento Econômico de Pernambuco, 1965.

Commons, John R. *Legal Foundations of Capitalism.* Madison: University of Wisconsin Press, 1957.

————. *Institutional Economics.* Madison: University of Wisconsin Press, 1959.

CONTAG. "Primeiro Encontro Regional dos Trabalhadores na Lavoura Canavieira do Nordeste." Mimeographed. Carpina, Pernambuco: Confederação Nacional dos Trabalhadores Agricolas, March 1967.

Cumberland, Charles C. *Mexico: The Struggle for Modernity.* New York: Oxford University Press, 1968.

da Costa, Emília Viotti. "O Escravo na Grande Lavoura." In *História Geral da Civilização Brasileira*, edited by Sérgio Buarque de Holanda. São Paulo: Difusão Européia do Livro, 1967.

Dantas, Bento. "A Margem do Encontro de Ocupação do Território." *Brasil Açucareiro*, January 1968.

Debray, Régis. *Revolution in the Revolution?* Translated by Bobbye Ortiz. New York: Grove Press, 1967.

Deer, Noël. *Cane Sugar.* Manchester: Norman Rodger, 1911.

————. *The History of Sugar*. London: Chapman & Hall, 1949.

Delgado, Oscar, ed. *Reformas Agrarias en la América Latina*. México: Fondo de Cultura Económica, 1965.

Diégues Junior, Manuel. *População e Propriedade da Terra no Brasil*. Washington: Pan American Union, 1959.

DNP. *O Açúcar sob o Governo Getulio Vargas*. Rio de Janeiro: Departamento Nacional da Propaganda, 1939.

do Rêgo, José Lins. *Plantation Boy*. Translated by Emmi Baum. New York: Alfred A. Knopf, 1966.

Estes, Sue Horn. "What the Poor Are Up Against in Texas." *New Republic*, July 19, 1969.

Felipe, Israel. *História do Cabo*. Recife: Imprensa Oficial, 1962.

Frank, Andre Gunder. "Mexico: The Janus Faces of 20th Century Bourgeois Revolution." In *Whither Latin America?*, edited by Paul M. Sweezy and Leo Huberman. New York: Monthly Review Press, 1963.

————. *Capitalism and Underdevelopment in Latin America: Historical Studies of Chile and Brazil*. New York: Monthly Review Press, 1967.

Freyre, Gilberto. *Nordeste: Aspectos da Influencia da Canna Sobre a Vida e a Paizagem do Nordeste do Brasil*. Rio de Janeiro: José Olympio, 1937.

Furtado, Celso. *The Economic Growth of Brazil*. Translated by Ricardo W. de Aguiar and Eric Charles Drysdale. Berkeley: University of California Press, 1963.

————. "Brazil: What Kind of Revolution?" In *Economic Development: Evolution or Revolution?*, edited by Laura Randall. Boston: D. C. Heath, 1964.

————. *Diagnosis of the Brazilian Crisis*. Translated by Suzette Macedo. Berkeley: University of California Press, 1965.

————. *Development and Underdevelopment*. Translated by Ricardo W. de Aguiar and Eric Charles Drysdale. Berkeley: University of California Press, 1967.

Galbraith, John Kenneth. "Conditions for Economic Change in Underdeveloped Countries." *Journal of Farm Economics*, November 1951.

Gambs, John S. *Beyond Supply and Demand: A Reappraisal of Institutional Economics*. New York: Columbia University Press, 1946.

GERAN. *Programa Estadual de Pernambuco*. Recife: Grupo Executívo da Racionalização da Agroindústria Açucareira do Nordeste, 1966.

Gonçalves, Fernando Antônio. "Condições de Vida do Trabalhador Rural da Zona da Mata do Estado de Pernambuco—1964." *Boletim do Instituto Joaquim Nabuco de Pesquisas Sociais*, no. 15, 1966.

Goulart, Mauricio. *Escravidão Africano no Brasil*. São Paulo: Livraria Martins Editôra, 1950.

Graham, Richard. "Causes for the Abolition of Negro Slavery in Brazil: An Interpretive Essay." *Hispanic American Historical Review*, May 1966.

Gray, Lewis Cecil. *History of Agriculture in the Southern United States to 1860*. Washington: Carnegie Institute, 1933.

Guerra y Sánchez, Ramiro. *Sugar and Society in the Caribbean*. New Haven: Yale University Press, 1964.

Hall, Douglas. *Free Jamaica, 1838–1865: An Economic History*. New Haven: Yale University Press, 1959.

Haring, C. H. *Empire in Brazil*. Cambridge: Harvard University Press, 1958.

Harlow, Vincent T. *A History of Barbados, 1625–1685*. Oxford: Clarendon Press, 1926.

Harris, Marvin. "Race Relations in Minas Velhas, a Community in the Mountain Region of Central Brazil." In *Race and Class in Rural Brazil*, edited by Charles Wagley. New York: UNESCO, 1963.

Hicks, J. R. *Essays in World Economics*. Oxford: Clarendon Press, 1959.

Hirschman, Albert O. *Journeys Toward Progress: Studies of Economic Policy-Making In Latin America*. New York: Twentieth Century Fund, 1963.

Hogen, Timothy L. *A Report on the Cooperative League in Northeastern Brazil*. Chicago: Cooperative League of the U.S.A., 1966.

Horowitz, Irving Louis. *Revolution in Brazil: Politics and Society in a Developing Nation*. New York: E. P. Dutton, 1964.

————. "The Norm of Illegitimacy: The Political Sociology of Latin America." In *Latin American Radicalism*, edited by Irving Louis Horowitz, Josué de Castro, and John Gerassi. New York: Vintage, 1969.

Huberman, Leo, and Paul M. Sweezy. *Socialism in Cuba*. New York: Monthly Review Press, 1969.

Hutchinson, Bertram. "The Migrant Population of Urban Brazil." *América Latina* 6, no. 2 (1963).

Hutchinson, Harry W. "Race Relations in a Rural Community of the Bahian Reconcave." In *Race and Class in Rural Brazil*, edited by Charles Wagely. New York: UNESCO, 1963.

IAA. *Boletim de Agosto, Safra de 1964 / 65*. Recife: Instituto do Açúcar e do Alcool, 1965.

Ibarguen, Roberto. "The War of Mascates, 1710–1715: Urbanizing Catalyst in the Development of Recife, Brazil." *Latinamericanist* (Gainesville, Fla.), February 15, 1969.

IBGE. *VII Recenseamento Geral do Brasil, 1960, Censo Demográfico, Resultados Preliminares*. Rio de Janeiro: Instituto Brasileiro de Geografia e Estatística, 1960.

ICNND. *Northeast Brazil: Nutrition Survey*. Washington: Interdepartmental Committee on Nutrition for National Development, 1965.

IJNPS. *Transformação Regional e Ciência Ecológica*. Recife: Instituto Joaquim Nabuco de Pesquisas Sociais, 1964.

————. *O Problema Agrário na Zona Canavieira de Pernambuco*. Recife: Instituto Joaquim Nabuco de Pesquisas Sociais, 1965.

Jaguaribe, Helio. *Economic and Political Development: A Theoretical Approach and a Brazilian Case Study*. Cambridge: Harvard University Press, 1968.

Joint Commission. *The Development of Brazil*. Washington: Joint Brazil–United States Economic Development Commission, 1954.

Jorgenson, Harold T. "Impending Disaster in Northeastern Brazil." *Inter-American Economic Affairs*, Summer 1968.

Koster, Henry. *Travels in Brazil*. Edited by C. Harvey Gardiner. Carbondale: Southern Illinois University Press, 1966.

Kurz, Peter. "Peasants and Politics in Northeastern Brazil." Senior thesis, Princeton University, 1964.

Lando, Barry. "News You Won't Find in Brazil's Newspapers." *New Republic*, August 2, 1969.

Leff, Nathaniel H. *Economic Policy-Making and Development in Brazil, 1947–1964*. New York: John Wiley & Sons, 1968.

Lewis, W. Arthur. "Economic Development with Unlimited Supplies of Labor." In *The Economics of Underdevelopment*, edited by A. N. Agarwala and S. P. Singh. New York: Oxford University Press, 1963.

Lima, Barbosa. *Problemas Econômicos e Sociais da Lavoura Canavieira*. Rio de Janeiro: Pimenta de Mello, 1941.

————. *Os Fundamentos Nacionais da Política do Açúcar*. Rio de Janeiro: Instituto do Açúcar e do Alcool, 1943.

Lippmann, Edmund O. von. *História do Açúcar*. Vol. 2. Translated by Rodolfo Coutinho. Rio de Janeiro: Instituto do Açúcar e do Alcool, 1942.

Maddox, James G. "Economic Growth and Revolution in Mexico." *Land Economics*, August 1960.
————. "La Revolución y la Reforma Agraria." In *Reformas Agrarias en la América Latina*, edited by Oscar Delgado. México: Fundo de Cultura Económica, 1965.
Magdoff, Harry. *The Age of Imperialism: The Economics of U.S. Foreign Policy*. New York: Monthly Review Press, 1969.
Manchester, Alan K. *British Preëminence in Brazil*. Chapel Hill: University of North Carolina Press, 1933.
Mandel, Ernest. *Marxist Economic Theory*. Translated by Brian Pearce. 2 vols. London: Monthly Review Press, 1968.
Marchant, Alexander. *From Barter to Slavery: The Economic Relations of Portuguese and Indians in the Settlement of Brazil*. Baltimore: Johns Hopkins University Press, 1942.
Marx, Karl. *Capital*. Translated by Samuel Moore and Edward Aveling, Kerr edition. New York: Random House, 1906.
Meany, George. *Not in Our Image*. Washington: American Institute for Free Labor Development, n.d.
Melo, Mário Lacerda de. *As Migrações para o Recife*. Vol. 1, *Estudo Geográfico*. Recife: Instituto Joaquim Nabuco de Pesquisas Sociais, 1961.
Mill, John Stuart. *Principles of Political Economy*. 2 vols. New York: D. Appleton and Company, 1897.
Myrdal, Gunnar. *Rich Lands and Poor: The Road to World Prosperity*. New York: Harper & Row, 1957.

North, Douglass C. "Agriculture in Regional Economic Growth." In *Agriculture and Economic Development*, edited by Carl Eicher and Lawrence Witt. New York: McGraw-Hill, 1964.
Nun, José. "A Latin American Phenomenon: The Middle-Class Military Coup." In *Latin America: Reform or Revolution?*, edited by James Petras and Maurice Zeitlin. Greenwich, Conn.: Fawcett, 1968.

OAS. *Marketing Problems of Sugar at the Hemisphere and World Levels*. Washington: Pan American Union, 1964.
O'Conner, James. "On Cuban Political Economy." In *Latin America: Reform or Revolution?*, edited by James Petras and Maurice Zeitlin. Greenwich, Conn.: Fawcett, 1968.
Oliveira, Hugo Paulo de. "Os Presidentes do I. A. A." *Brasil Açucareiro*, November 1968.

Page, Joseph A. *The Revolution that Never Was: Northeast Brazil, 1955–1964*. New York: Grossman, 1972.
Parry, J. H., and P. M. Sherlock. *A Short History of the West Indies*. New York: St. Martin's Press, 1965.
Pearson, Neal John. "Small Farmer and Rural Worker Pressure Groups in Brazil." Ph.D. dissertation, University of Florida, 1967.
Pinheiro, Tobias. "Lei Aurea Liquidou com os Engenhos de Minha Terra." *Brasil Açucareiro*, June 1967.
Poppino, Rollie E. *Brazil: The Land and People*. New York: Oxford University Press, 1968.
Prado Júnior, Caio. *The Colonial Background of Modern Brazil*. Translated by Suzette Macedo. Berkeley: University of California Press, 1967.
Prebisch, Raúl. "The Economic Development of Latin America and Its Principal Problems." *Economic Bulletin for Latin America*, February 1962.

Recenseamento Geral do Brasil. Rio de Janeiro: Conselho Nacional de Estatística, 1956.
Ricardo, David. *The Principles of Political Economy and Taxation*. New York: E. P. Dutton & Co., 1960.
Robinson, Joan. *Economic Philosophy*. Chicago: Aldine, 1963.

————. *The Economics of Imperfect Competition*. New York: St. Martin's Press, 1965.

Robock, Stefan H. *Brazil's Developing Northeast*. Washington: Brookings Institution, 1963.

Rosa e Silva Neto, J. M. da. *Contribuição ao Estudo da Zona da Mata em Pernambuco*. Recife: Instituto Joaquim Nabuco de Pesquisas Sociais, 1966.

Rostow, W. W. *The Stages of Economic Growth: A Non-Communist Manifesto*. Cambridge: Cambridge University Press, 1961.

St. Petersburg Times, April 15, 1969.

Schumpeter, Joseph A. *Imperialism and Social Classes*. Edited by Paul M. Sweezy. New York: Augustus M. Kelley, 1951.

Simonsen, Roberto C. *História Econômica do Brasil, 1500–1820*. São Paulo: Companhia Editôra Nacional, 1957.

Singer, H. W. "The Distribution of Gains Between Investing and Borrowing Countries." *American Economic Review*, May 1949.

Skidmore, Thomas E. *Politics in Brazil, 1930–1964: An Experiment in Democracy*. New York: Oxford University Press, 1967.

Slater, Charles, et al. *Market Processes in the Recife Area of Northeast Brazil*. Michigan State University Marketing in Developing Countries series. East Lansing: Michigan State University, 1969.

Smith, Adam. *An Inquiry into the Nature and Causes of the Wealth of Nations*. Edited by Edwin Cannan. New York: Random House, 1937.

Smith, T. Lynn. *Brazil: People and Institutions*. Baton Rouge: Louisiana State University Press, 1963.

Soares, Glaucio Ary Dillon. "The New Industrialization and the Brazilian Political System." In *Latin America: Reform or Revolution?*, edited by James Petras and Maurice Zeitlin. Greenwich, Conn.: Fawcett, 1968.

Sombart, Werner. *The Jews and Modern Capitalism*. Translated by M. Epstein. New York: Collier, 1962.

Stavenhagen, Rodolfo. "Seven Fallacies About Latin America." In *Latin America: Reform or Revolution?*, edited by James Petras and Maurice Zeitlin. Greenwich, Conn.: Fawcett, 1968.

Stein, Stanley J. *The Brazilian Cotton Manufacture*. Cambridge: Harvard University Press, 1957.

SUDENE. *Zoneamento Agrícola e Pecuário do Nordeste*. Mimeographed. Recife: Superintendência do Desenvolvimento do Nordeste, 1964.

Swerling, Boris C., and Vladimir P. Timoshenko. *The World's Sugar*. Stanford: Stanford University Press, 1957.

Szulc, Tad. "Northeast Brazil Poverty Breeds Threat of Revolt." *New York Times*, October 31, November 1, 1960.

Taunay, Affonso de E. *Subsídios para a História do Tráfico Africano no Brasil Colonial*. Rio de Janeiro: Instituto Histórico, 1941.

Veblen, Thorstein. *The Instinct of Workmanship*. New York: Macmillan, 1914.

Visão. Various issues.

Vitale, Luis. "Latin America: Feudal or Capitalist?" In *Latin America: Reform or Revolution?*, edited by James Petras and Maurice Zeitlin. Greenwich, Conn.: Fawcett, 1968.

Wagley, Charles. "From Caste to Class in North Brazil." In *Race and Class in Rural Brazil*, edited by Charles Wagley. New York: UNESCO, 1963.

Wakefield, Edward Gibbon. *England and America: A Comparison of the Social and Political State of Both Nations*. New York: Augustus M. Kelley, 1967.

Weber, Max. *The Theory of Social and Economic Organization*. Translated by A. M. Henderson and Talcott Parsons. Glencoe: Free Press, 1947.

Weeks, David. "The Agrarian System of the Spanish American Colonies." *The Journal of Land & Public Utility Economics*, May 1947.

Wharton, C. R., Jr. "Economic Meaning of Subsistence." *Malayan Economic Review*, October 1963.

Whittaker, Edmund. *Schools and Streams of Economic Thought*. Chicago: Rand McNally, 1960.

Williams, Eric. *Capitalism and Slavery*. New York: Capricorn, 1966.

Youmans, Russell, and G. Edward Schuh. "An Empirical Study of the Agricultural Labor Market in a Developing Country, Brazil." *Journal of Agricultural Economics*, November 1968.

Zimmerman, Ben. "Race Relations in the Arid Sertão." In *Race and Class in Rural Brazil*, edited by Charles Wagley. New York: UNESCO, 1963.

UNIVERSITY OF FLORIDA MONOGRAPHS

Social Sciences

1. *The Whigs of Florida, 1845–1854*, by Herbert J. Doherty, Jr.

2. *Austrian Catholics and the Social Question, 1918–1933*, by Alfred Diamant

3. *The Siege of St. Augustine in 1702*, by Charles W. Arnade

4. *New Light on Early and Medieval Japanese Historiography*, by John A. Harrison

5. *The Swiss Press and Foreign Affairs in World War II*, by Frederick H. Hartmann

6. *The American Militia: Decade of Decision, 1789–1800*, by John K. Mahon

7. *The Foundation of Jacques Maritain's Political Philosophy*, by Hwa Yol Jung

8. *Latin American Population Studies*, by T. Lynn Smith

9. *Jacksonian Democracy on the Florida Frontier*, by Arthur W. Thompson

10. *Holman Versus Hughes: Extension of Australian Commonwealth Powers*, by Conrad Joyner

11. *Welfare Economics and Subsidy Programs*, by Milton Z. Kafoglis

12. *Tribune of the Slavophiles: Konstantin Aksokov*. by Edward Chmielewski

13. *City Managers in Politics: An Analysis of Manager Tenure and Termination*, by Gladys M. Kammerer, Charles D. Farris, John M. DeGrove, and Alfred B. Clubok

14. *Recent Southern Economic Development as Revealed by the Changing Structure of Employment*, by Edgar S. Dunn, Jr.

15. *Sea Power and Chilean Independence*, by Donald E. Worcester

16. *The Sherman Antitrust Act and Foreign Trade*, by Andre Simmons

17. *The Origins of Hamilton's Fiscal Policies*, by Donald F. Swanson

18. *Criminal Asylum in Anglo-Saxon Law*, by Charles H. Riggs, Jr.

19. *Colonia Barón Hirsch, A Jewish Agricultural Colony in Argentina*, by Morton D. Winsberg

20. *Time Deposits in Present-Day Commercial Banking*, by L. L. Crum

21. *The Eastern Greenland Case in Historical Perspective*, by Oscar Svarlien

22. *Jacksonian Democracy and the Historians*, by Alfred A. Cave

23. *The Rise of the American Chemistry Profession, 1850–1900*, by Edward H. Beardsley

24. *Aymara Communities and the Bolivian Agrarian Reform*, by William E. Carter

25. *Conservatives in the Progressive Era: The Taft Republicans of 1912*, by Norman M. Wilensky

26. *The Anglo-Norwegian Fisheries Case of 1951 and the Changing Law of the Territorial Sea*, by Teruo Kobayashi

27. *The Liquidity Structure of Firms and Monetary Economics*, by William J. Frazer, Jr.

28. *Russo-Persian Commercial Relations, 1828–1914*, by Marvin L. Entner

29. *The Imperial Policy of Sir Robert Borden*, by Harold A. Wilson

30. *The Association of Income and Educational Achievement*, by Roy L. Lassiter, Jr.

31. *Relation of the People to the Land in Southern Iraq*, by Fuad Baali

32. *The Price Theory of Value in Public Finance*, by Donald R. Escarraz

33. *The Process of Rural Development in Latin America*, by T. Lynn Smith

34. *To Be or Not to Be . . . Existential-Psychological Perspectives on the Self*, edited by Sidney M. Jourard